book
of ideas

A journal of creative direction
and graphic design

Radim Malinic

Volume 2

 **Brand Nu®**

First published in the United Kingdom in 2018 by
Brand Nu Limited, www.brandnu.co.uk

Book of Ideas - A journal of creative direction
and graphic design ©2018 Radim Malinic

1 2 3 4 5 6 7 8 9 10 / 22 21 20 19 18

Written and designed by Radim Malinic
Editorial assistance by Greg Browne
Copyediting by Emily Gosling

All showcase images and photos by
©Brand Nu unless otherwise stated.

British Library Cataloguing-in-Publication Data
A catalogue record for this book is available
from the British Library

ISBN 978-0-9935400-1-1

Proudly printed and bound in
England by Taylor Bloxham

350gsm GalerieArt Satin - FSC Mix
100gsm UPM Fine Offset - FSC Mix

To find out more about this publication or the author,
please visit brandnu.co.uk or bookofideas.co.uk

Volume 2

BOOK OF IDEAS / CONTENTS

/ WORK

BRAND STORIES _ **16**

REVERSE ENGINEERING _ **18**

BUILDING THE BASKET _ **20**

FREEDOM IN LIMITATIONS _ **24**

THE 'BIG BREAK' _ **26**

STARTING AFRESH, EVERY TIME _ **28**

SOCIAL MEDIA CAREERS _ **32**

THE FUNNEL OF OUTPUT _ **34**

STRESS TESTING _ **36**

NOTHING IS EVER LOST _ **40**

THE BOX OF MACAROONS _ **42**

MAKING THINGS HAPPEN ON THE GO _ **44**

DREAM CLIENTS _ **48**

STOP / START PRODUCTIVITY _ **50**

THE PROBLEM WITH 'YESTERDAY' _ **52**

/ CASE STUDIES

VISUAL STORYTELLING _ **56**

DESIGNING FOR SEASONS _ **62**

FOOD FOR THOUGHT _ **70**

OPPOSITES ATTRACT _ **76**

MAKING DATA LOOK GREAT _ **84**

INTRODUCTION _ **10**

GETTING STARTED WITH ADOBE STOCK _ **244**

MAKING OF THE BOOK COVER _ **246**

ABOUT THE AUTHOR _ **252**

THANKS & ACKNOWLEDGEMENTS _ **254**

For my daughter
Harper Lux Freda

BOOK OF IDEAS - VOL.2
THIS IS A JOURNAL OF
STORIES, LEARNINGS AND
MUSINGS GARNERED FROM
THE DAY-TO-DAY RUNNING OF
A CREATIVE BUSINESS WITH
THE SIMPLE AIM TO PRODUCE
THE BEST POSSIBLE WORK.
THIS BOOK WON'T TEACH YOU
TO HOW DESIGN, BUT IT SHOULD
SHOW YOU HOW YOU CAN BE
A BETTER AND MORE THOUGHTFUL
DESIGNER, CREATOR AND THINKER
BY RADIM MALINIC

/ CREATIVITY

AMBITION V REALITY _ 94

SAY LITTLE TO SAY A LOT _ 96

FIND (AND BE) A MENTOR _ 98

AN INFLUENTIAL COMMUNITY _ 120

EXPLORE YOUR SILLY _ 104

GALLERY V HIGH STREET _ 106

A CORRIANDER STORY _ 110

CRACKING YOUR CREATIVE DNA _ 112

CONSCIOUS CREATIVITY _ 114

THE RIGHT WRONG _ 118

LEARNING TO FLY _ 120

WHY VS HOW _ 122

SPEAKING THE LANGUAGE _ 130

WHAT DOES CREATIVITY MEAN TO YOU? _ 132

CREATIVITY FOR FREE? _ 134

/ CASE STUDIES

MIND THE GAP _ 136

TWO HOURS TO CHANGE FUTURE _ 144

COKE + ADOBE + YOU _ 152

AM:PM PM:AM _ 158

WHAT COLOUR CAN YOU HEAR? _ 164

/ MIND

MAKE RULES, FOLLOW THEM _ 170

CREATIVE ATHLETE _ 172

KNOW YOUR ENEMY WITHIN _ 174

WANT TO BE FAMOUS? THINK AGAIN _ 178

POWER OF QUIET _ 180

REPEAT, REPEAT, REPEAT _ 182

THE ART OF LETTING GO _ 186

EVERY DAY DIFFERENT _ 188

ON STAYING HUMBLE _ 190

LESSONS IN COMPASSION _ 194

BE HERE NOW _ 196

SLEEP WHEN YOU SLEEP, WORK WHEN YOU WORK _ 198

YOU ARE WHO YOU SHOULD BE _ 202

INVENT YOUR DREAM FUTURE _ 204

SEASONS CHANGE _ 206

/ CASE STUDIES

STILLNESS + TIME _ 210

WHERE THE CITY STOPS _ 218

OBJECTS IN SPACE _ 226

THIS IS NOT A GYM _ 230

THE COLOURS OF MOODS _ 236

Volume 2

BOOK OF IDEAS / INTRODUCTION

This book is a journal of stories, learnings and musings garnered from the day-to-day running of a creative business with the simple aim to produce the best possible work.

Book of Ideas Volume 2 broadly shares its predecessor's structure, set around the Work, Creativity and Mind sections, though this time around there are added case studies that each serve to illustrate certain chapters, or "ideas", with explanations around how and why they were made.

Many years ago when I took stock of my career so far, I came to the realisation that I was mostly average in everything that I had done so far – I was far from making the best of the time we have on earth. That led to a conscious decision to step up in every aspect of my life and work, and I've been on a quest ever since to become a less distracted and generally better designer, director, speaker and human being.

A couple of years ago, I became a parent. I'm a proud father to a beautiful girl who now rules my world. Soon came the first baby steps, words and smiles. She's now at the defiant, unruly toddler stage, where she sometimes cries when she wants something, gets what she wanted, and shouts back that it's actually not what she wanted at all. When that gets taken away, she shouts again and asks for it back. Ah, the terrible twos.

That behaviour reminds me of how client work sometimes pans out – it seems the toddler stage is never truly left behind in adulthood. Producing creative work can occasionally feel like trying to serve dinner to an uninterested toddler who has instantly developed an overwhelming dislike of their once-favourite food. All that effort goes to waste.

Creativity isn't meant to be easy – we need a healthy balance of struggle and reward to keep us interested, to keep coming back. However, it's not meant to be impossible, and we have to keep the balance between failures and victories along the way, signs we're making headway.

A mountain climber might struggle all the way to the summit, but when they reach it, that effort is rewarded. They learned to perfect their skills and craft to get better at what they do. I see the world of creativity in the same way, even though it's meant to come with fewer blisters and bruises.

This is why I believe we need to be constantly striving toward better efficiency in how we conduct the exchange of creative energy. Those who just run into the same problems time and time again have only themselves to blame: we have to learn from every mistake or argument. Online resources can teach you pretty much any software or skill, and you can watch countless "inspirational" TED talks with big ideas, but it really depends on the individual to implement their learnings.

Taking time to reflect what you've done, or what you're doing right now, is hugely important. The ones who succeed don't just plough ahead aimlessly without really thinking about it: they have a map, a plan and the grit to keep going until they get to where they want to.

I believe most of the people who get into the creative industries did so for the belief that they can change the world in some capacity – we can learn so much from the vast legacy of those before us, who were trying to make sense of it all for a better future. Many job roles today didn't exist a decade ago: we're riding a wave of innovation, revolution and technological advances at an unprecedented speed. Everything is changing, yet most of the time we're still trying to catch up on such changes from yesterday, a week ago or even years before.

I believe that everyone can be a multifaceted "creative athlete" who goes for their personal best every single day. Every day should be a gold medal opportunity.

Much of that might come down to improving how we communicate, starting with looking at simple ways of talking more effectively about what we create, as well as nurturing compassion for people around us. It's about taking time to reset our thought patterns and get into the best frame of mind to take on the world.

When you're standing on the train platform with a thousand silent strangers, it's an opportunity to focus your mind on that very minute and observe the world around you. Focus on your breathing and get ready to have an amazing day.

Within these pages, you'll find anecdotes aplenty, words of encouragement and advice on how to navigate client situations and projects, and advice on how to find the most enjoyment in everything that's presented to you. The prevalent underlying theme is staying in the present moment, focusing on what you do. Only by doing so you will be able to find the true excitement in what you do and make.

This book won't teach you to how design, but it should show you how you can be a better and more thoughtful designer, thinker and creator. I hope you can find something in here to point you in the right direction.

Thank you for taking the time to read this book.

WORK

When creative work goes well, it's the stuff the dreams are made of; when it goes badly, it's a nightmare.

To improve your process, you have to question it. The **Work** section looks into ways of working and planning, how to stir the right reactions in your work proposals, embracing the power of limitation over endless choice and in doing so, how to provide holistic design work with confidence.

BRAND STORIES

When we're interested in an artist, we study their body of work, listen to their albums, visit their galleries and work our way through their back catalogue.

We want to know everything: where they grew up, where they studied, and even who they dated – every nuance of their life. The best creative campaigns know the importance of those stories. It's up to us to take seemingly ordinary stories and make them into magical tales that everyone wants to hear.

When we're challenged to create a new object of desire in the shape of a brand, product or service, we have to convince both sides of the equation: the client and their customer.

This means making work that's visually engaging, but backed up with a full creative narrative – a long-term proposition built up from many intricate stories.

We want to uncover the brand's existing DNA or find a way to form new stories. So many new brands are inventing their supposed origins to portray their roots, values or vision for the future. These become their mission statements. But we always have to ask: "what's their reason to exist?"

Show clients why they should care. Show customers why they should stick around. What is it that you're trying to say? What journey are you taking people on, and where are you taking them?

The most powerful brand stories stop people in their tracks and draw them in. We need to create those tales that become irresistible, that make people want to study every little detail and turn them into legions of dedicated fans.

REVERSE ENGINEERING

My friend Glen is a long distance runner and a bit of crazy guy who likes to put his body through its paces. When we chat about his latest marathon, I like to discuss the details of how he managed to go the distance; and I soon realised his race doesn't begin at the starting line, it starts right at the end. In his preparation, he goes back to front and works out the pace and timing versus the terrain and elevation to make sure he can get to where he wants to be in the best time possible. It makes perfect sense.

Just as you put the end destination into a sat nav, we should think about the end of the journey from the start. You work out how much time you need and what the journey looks like, so you can plan for any fuel stops along the way and check in with yourself to make sure it's all going ok.

This is how you should tackle new client enquiries and projects. When people get in touch, they're usually focused on the immediate problem and rarely look beyond it.

When we get lost on a car journey, we think of taking any side route possible to get back on track. We start to panic, which doesn't help. Instead, cut the faffing, take a deep breath and look at the map.

Look at it as "reverse engineering" when working out where someone's idea should end up. We like to spot the "gap in the market" or the "golden opportunity", but to achieve those propositions you need a plan, map and the tools to help you get there. That's why working backwards can be the best and most helpful way to devise a plan to move forward. Where others might want to make a hasty head start, it pays to take the time to observe the problem objectively and consider the most enjoyable and effective way to tackle it.

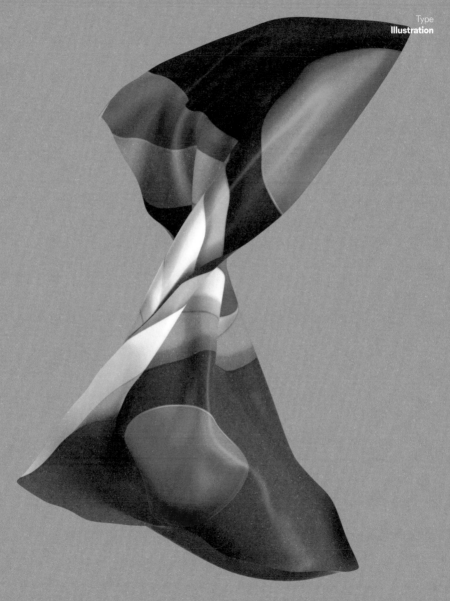

BUILDING THE BASKET

When you pop to the shops for a pint of milk, it's likely you'll find it towards the back of the store. That's part logistics, part clever retailer psychology: to get to what you need, you'll have to pass the other things you don't think you want, but might pick up anyway. They make you build up a full basket.

This is a good analogy for branding and design: countless clients might just be after a metaphorical pint of milk – a logo, business card or app icon – but a brand can't survive on milk (or a logo) alone. You need other ingredients to make a decent breakfast.

I've been using the term "basket" for a while now, but it's important people realise you're not just hoodwinking them into buying things they don't need. There are numerous components that form a brand's whole and make it a success. Indeed, the logo plays the main part, but it wouldn't be half as useful without a supporting cast of brand assets: solid brand font usage, colour themes, wayfinding icons, brand illustrations, brochures, stationery, templates for social media posts, online banners, packaging design and so much more that serves as a brand toolkit and usage guidelines. That might not always be clear to somebody outside of the design process.

Your ability to convince a client of the value of a more holistic approach will determine whether you get to do the big-boy work you've always dreamed of doing, or if you'll be forever waiting for the "perfect" client to come along and give you the green light.

When people know you've got their back – that you want them to take home the best stuff on offer – they can enjoy the creative process with you, and stop worrying about the "value" of design.

Client
The Green Den

Type
**Branding
+ Design**

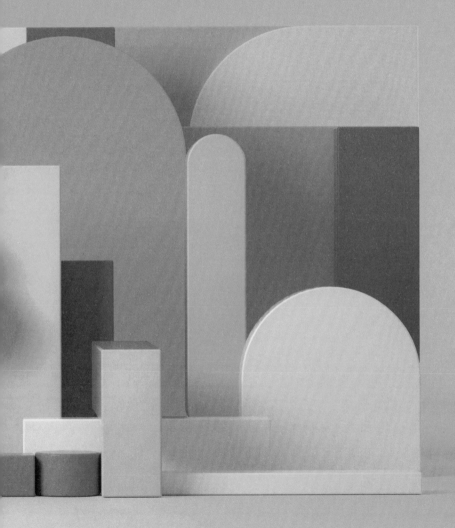

FREEDOM IN LIMITATIONS

Creative freedom might seem like the ultimate halcyon dream.
But we crave many things, and not all of them good for us: sugar,
nicotine, caffeine, crap TV, and so on. But just like sugar, creative
freedom can be sweet but ultimately corrosive when we have
it too often.

Too much choice is a killer of good ideas, joy and productivity:
a never-ending stream of options is a surefire way to dull interest
in any of them. We are much more content making choices from
fewer options, rather than many. When you can choose two scoops
of ice cream from two dozen flavours, you spend most of the time
thinking about the flavours you didn't choose. When there's only
half a dozen to choose from, we're far more likely to feel we made
the right decision. I speak from my own gelato-based experience.

Creative freedom sounds like fun, but it makes it hard to ever
be totally satisfied: you might never know when a piece of work
is actually finished as you doggedly tweak it until the small hours
and ultimately lose sight of the end goal. Such freedom is great for
artists, but often too much for designers.

Working within limitations is the key to making work that is not
only enjoyable but more effective at making connections with
those it was created for. You need to learn how to focus on
the right idea and validate the concept before making the decision
of what to pitch, propose and create. Cut down your options until
you know that you can confidently choose an art direction that
works properly, and carve out a space in which
to make great work.

The limitation doesn't mean cutting the fun out of design work:
it makes the process all the sweeter. The biggest privilege
of your career is the freedom to choose your limitations.

Select Currency GBP $

COLLECTIONS   TOYS & GAMES   PRINTS   ENTERTAINMENT   EXPERIENCES   BY FILM   MORE   007.COM

FRAGRANCES

NEW IN

NEW IN

JAMES BOND 007 COLOGNE
50ML
£24.95

JAMES BOND 007 COLOGNE
30ML
£21.95

JAMES BOND 007 WOMEN II EAU
DE PARFUM 75ML
£33.99

JAMES BOND 007 WOMEN II EAU
DE PARFUM 50ML
£25.99

JAMES BOND 007 WOMEN II EAU
DE PARFUM 30ML
£18.99

JAMES BOND 007 WOMEN III EAU
DE PARFUM 75ML
£33.99

JAMES BOND 007 WOMEN III EAU
DE PARFUM 50ML
£25.99

JAMES BOND 007 WOMEN III EAU
DE PARFUM 30ML
£18.99

007 FOR WOMEN III BODY LOTION
150ML
£7.99

JAMES BOND 007 SIGNATURE
EAU DE TOILETTE 125ML
£44.99

JAMES BOND 007 SIGNATURE
EAU DE TOILETTE 75ML
£32.00

JAMES BOND 007 SIGNATURE
EAU DE TOILETTE 50ML
£25.00

Newsletter Sign up

Latest News, Launches and Offers

Enter name   Your email address   >

☐ I agree   ☐ I disagree

to receive emails from the 007Store to receive offers and promotions I might be interested in.

You have the right to withdraw your consent at any time, by clicking 'unsubscribe' in an email
confirmation that you will soon receive and in any of our communications with you. This will
remove your email address from our databases. Opt out at any time by sending email to
orders@the007store.com or by unsubscribing via a link in the email. By clicking on the
Submit button, I acknowledge that I have read and understand the Privacy Policy.

Useful Information
About Us
My Account
Privacy Policy
Terms and Conditions
Cookie Policy

Help
FAQs
Contact
Shipping and Delivery
Refunds and Exchanges

THE 'BIG BREAK'

Any career – creative or otherwise – is a marathon, not a sprint.
We have fleeting goals and long-term dreams: if we just rush towards the former, the latter will prove harder to reach. The term "there's no such thing as an overnight success" is a cliche because it's true.

We're led to believe that a new music act is breaking onto the scene right this second, even though a label has had them holed up in the studio for years working out the release plan, sound and marketing strategy. In the world of tech, many of the leading "startups" are nearing their ten year anniversaries, despite the fact most of us are blissfully unaware of their existence. They've likely been hovering around the failure level before things start to happen. Success is rooted in persistence, effort and patience.

The development of a design career seems to be a lot less dramatic and tumultuous, but that doesn't stop us from wanting to make waves, now. When we see our peers and other studios working with bigger projects, it pushes us to try harder and take things up a level.

When I left my last full-time job to go freelance, it took a while for the bigger work to come. I promoted the hell out of my portfolio, I contacted everyone I wanted to work for and with, and I made sure I was always pushing myself forward. The efforts paid dividends.

Little did I envisage that bigger projects would entail more input, effort and time. When you step into that world, no one asks if you're able to deliver what they want – there's no time. Such work can be relentless and all-consuming, and getting to the good stuff isn't easy.

It's hard to define a "big break" and how to get it: that differs from person to person. Some might not be interested, others will seek it obsessively. But if you produce good, honest work, bigger opportunities will come your way sooner rather than later.

Client
Cursed Child store

Type
Graphic design

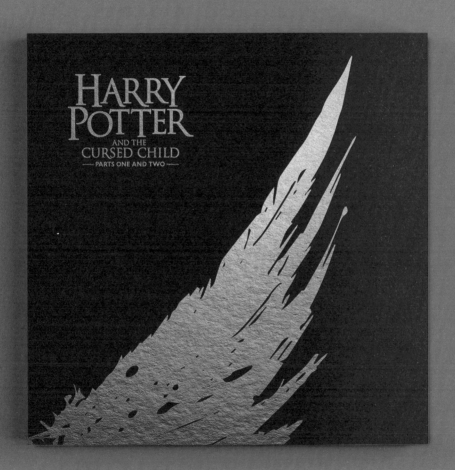

STARTING AFRESH, EVERY TIME

Commissions, projects and clients come in all shapes and sizes, each with unique requirements that deserve equally unique solutions. While many branding clients will bring their own story and company history, it's important to look into things with a fresh perspective: clear the clutter and examine every part of the story.

It's incredibly valuable to look at a brand's history to see what parts of their past to bring into the next chapter. The best new ideas are often rooted in the values that have long contributed to the success of the business, and we can build on those foundations to further elevate our concept.

We all have something of a signature style and certain go-to techniques that make us stand out. You might be discouraged from trying to reinvent the wheel by many people around you who deem it impossible, expensive, or worst of all, unnecessary. But where would we be if we always tried to play it safe?

Every single time a wheel is being "reinvented" (or at least improved), something new arrives thanks to the courage, determination and passion of those tinkering with it.

Whether you run a freelance business or you're part of an agency, every new person, client or project that comes through your door is bound to be unique.

We should do our utmost to keep them that way.

Store Locator   Store Information   Log In / Register   Help   Your Cart (1)
£16.99

ONLINE STORE
HARRY POTTER
AND THE CURSED CHILD
~~~~ PARTS ONE AND TWO ~~~~
BASED ON AN ORIGINAL NEW STORY BY J.K. ROWLING, JACK THORNE & JOHN TIFFANY
A NEW PLAY BY JACK THORNE

Apparel   Souvenirs   Wands   Books   Search:

NEW *Official Cursed Child Merchandise*

Cursed Child T-shirt
Official Cursed Child Merchandise

£30.00

SIZE   S M L   XL   Size Guide and Care Guide

A t-shirt featuring the Harry Potter and the Cursed Child show logo in gold. Back of t-shirt displays the name of the Lyric Theatre, New York.

| ADD TO BAG | ADD TO WISHLIST |

RETURNS   DELIVERY

SHARE: f t t   FREE DELIVERY OVER £50

YOU MAY ALSO LIKE

Cursed Child T-shirt One   Cursed Child T-shirt One   Cursed Child T-shirt One   Cursed Child T-shirt One
£16.99   £16.99   £16.99   £16.99

Information	Here to Help	Shop with Us	Find Us
ABOUT	DELIVERY	CONTACT US	Cursed Child Shop
STORE LOCATION	RETURNS POLICY	CUSTOMER SERVICES	at The Palace Theatre
CAREERS	STORE OPENING HOURS	TERMS & CONDITIONS	113 Shaftesbury Ave,
ETHICAL TRADE	FAQS	PRIVACY POLICY	London W1D 5AY

Pottermore
from J.K. Rowling
WW

PALACE THEATRE
SHAFTESBURY AVENUE, LONDON W1D 5AY

FIND US ON t f ◎ t

Client
**Newton
Wakeham
Kibworth**

Type
**Branding
+ Design**

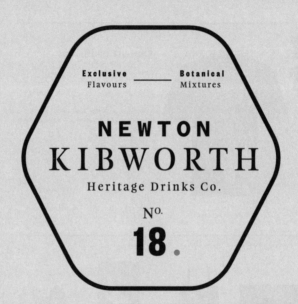

SOCIAL MEDIA CAREERS

For those in the creative industries, social media can feel like a big pond that's becoming increasingly crowded: you're just a little fish swimming alongside plumbers, cake-making hobbyists, insurance ads and billions of other people. You sputter out daily posts and quietly hope something will bubble to the surface.

Many believe that social media presence is an integral part of a successful career. But is it really the place a marketing director is going to look for the talent to rebrand a huge company? Just imagine the conversation between the CEO and the CMO when they get told the designer was found on Facebook: 'John, this designer has got 500 followers, likes vegan food and their cat looks super cool, let's hire him over the design firm with 20 years' experience'.

We're slaves to the many different algorithms that apparently control these spaces. We don't need to see any more images of a perfect cappuccino dusted with leaf-shaped chocolate sprinkles coupled with a motivational message written in chalkboard script.

We need to value each other's time while understanding that real creative careers are still very much created off-screen when you get your hands dirty. Apps are just there to broadcast the good stuff that you have.

Even the most influential "influencers" have to work offline to create something tangible. I'd love to see a day where the number of likes and followers gets hidden or removed – when everyone would become equal. Surely the dopamine hit from just being on a level playing field would match that of counting extra likes and follows.

Don't rely on other people's apps and websites to work for you. People have been making great, honest and wholesome work for hundreds of years, and it's worked perfectly. The means of getting it out into the world have expanded, but the purpose stays the same: to communicate visually through doing your best.

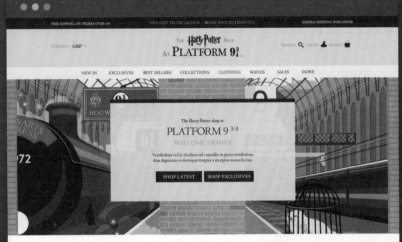

FREE SHIPPING ON ORDERS OVER £40   NEW GIFT TRUNK LAUNCH · 01 DAY 5 HOURS 2 MINUTES   EXPRESS SHIPPING WORLDWIDE

THE **Harry Potter** SHOP
AT **PLATFORM 9¾**

CURRENCY **GBP** ▾   SEARCH 🔍   LOGIN 👤   BASKET 🛍

NEW IN   EXCLUSIVES   BEST SELLERS   COLLECTIONS   CLOTHING   WANDS   SALES   MORE

The Harry Potter shop at

PLATFORM 9 ¾
WELCOME ABOARD!

Vestibulum sed ac facilisis vel convallis in porta vestibulum duis dignissim scelerisque tempus a inceptos massa lectus.

SHOP LATEST   **SHOP EXCLUSIVES**

Exlusive
'COLLECTION'
SPOTLIGHT SPACE

Vestibulum sed ac facilisis vel convallis in porta vestibulum duis dignissim scelerisque tempus a inceptos massa lectus.

GIFT IDEAS   **COLLECTIONS**

Exlusives
NEW SCHOOL TRUNKS
NOW IN!

Vestibulum sed ac facilisis vel convallis in porta vestibulum duis dignissim scelerisque tempus a inceptos massa lectus.

PRODUCT LINK   **COLLECTION**

● ○ ○ ○

Exclusive edition
MARAUDERS MAP
SHOP NOW

Just Arrived
NEW IN
SHOP NOW

THE FUNNEL OF OUTPUT

I see the creative process as the shape of an old-fashioned egg timer. The top of our egg timer symbolises the time you spend looking into understanding who you work for: their hopes and fears, competition, how they make their product, where they sell it and to whom.

You throw market research references together, look at type styles, shapes and colours, smells and sounds, personalities and odd characteristics, values and strategy: everything that makes up the brand and informs the idea you can take forward. The more time you spend feeding that top section, the more likely it is that your idea will become something that will connect with people when you launch your project.

The narrow middle section is all about making decisions. This is where you show the world the big idea. All the time you've spent on research should come good at this stage. You no longer entertain five different routes, you've found the one that you're going to run with. You're good to go. Or are you?

How daring are you going to be with the next step of the application? The bottom part of the egg timer contains the same amount of space as the top. It symbolises the endless possibilities of how big we can now grow our idea, using all that was learned in the research stages to inform the vision for all the assets created next. We have every chance to build dynamic systems that keep clients and their customers excited.

The only limitation could be our own skillset, but remember there's always someone out there who can help you to collaborate and elevate your idea even higher. This is why we spend so much time at the beginning of the process to show us the way forward. Just like the egg timer shape suggests, you spent equal time and energy on both parts. They both depend on and complement each other.

STRESS TESTING

There's a saying in architecture that no one will let you build a house unless you've already built one. As with anything, people want to see what you're capable of before they can trust you. Thanks to CGI modelling, there's a way around that: building designs can be created digitally to present to the public, creating an opportunity for people to make an emotional connection before the structure is built.

Graphic design is no different: while our creations are smaller in scale, we still have to convince people of their worth before we build them. We have to be clever with how we present work to get the green light – it has to be understood to be approved.

Through digital mockups, it's easier than ever to make even the most unimaginative client understand what we want to do before a single thing goes to print. Design stress testing helps to validate your creations and gives you a feel of how your designs work with the dynamics of the spaces they'll be applied to.

It's invaluable to you both as a creative and to your clients. A logo alone can look great, but might fall flat when you apply it across stationery or other touchpoints; so test them all, rigorously.

How does it work as the start of a bigger picture?

When you present a branding project, ad campaign, clothing line or anything else, you want to be one step ahead by covering all the possible options around where the project might go next.

Enjoy exploring every direction before you settle on the final option to show your clients. When you do, they'll love seeing the broader possibilities of how the designs could be applied.

Client
Hartridges

Type
**Packaging
development**

Client
Hartridges

Type
**Packaging
development**

Client
Hartridges

Type
**Packaging
development**

NOTHING IS EVER LOST

Life is made up of a series of moments – good and bad.
Work is the same. There will be times when things you worked tirelessly on are rejected, occasionally for what seems like no good reason. Sadly, that's just the reality of being commissioned for creative work: no one will ever have a 100% success rate. It's worth bearing that in mind when you feel like you've been punched in the stomach in the wake of having your work scrapped. This doesn't mean you're a failure in any way – but it can dent your confidence.

While some people just bluntly blurt out their initial response, others communicate less-than-positive feedback well: they can be honest, constructive and supportive about the work that didn't meet the brief or expected standard. My best memory of such a moment was when an art director started a feedback session by praising every part of an illustration for an advertising campaign. When she went into the list of changes, I gradually realised that there wasn't anything they would keep from my original work. It was a roller coaster; I'd never come across such a process before or since. But I came out of the meeting excited about starting afresh. However, this is the exception that proves the rule. Many people who commission creative work aren't necessarily equipped with the knowledge of the process that goes into every piece of work. Just like I don't know how many other professions operate, I try to approach any feedback from the viewpoint of a designer: clear and measured.

When you get negative news about something you slaved away at for days on end, it's important to remind yourself that the law of averages sometimes has to come into play. You win some, you lose some. The more we learn about our craft and ourselves, the more we gain the skills to deal with rejection and negative feedback. We teach ourselves to be resilient and keep going, no matter what.

Don't let poor feedback dent your confidence. Most of the time there's no right or wrong in what we do: we have our own visions that we try to align with those of others. Remember that nothing is ever lost – there's always another day to get it right. Keep your chin up.

Client
Hashmats Health

Type
**Packaging
design**

HASHMATS®
HEALTH

BEST BEFORE

PIP CODE
406-6146

DIRECTIONS:
Recommended for
Adults and Children
over 12 years of age:
take **ONE** tablet per
day with your meal.
Swallow with water
or a cold drink. Not
to be chewed. To
be taken on a full
stomach.

A-Z
MULTIVITAMINS

Everyday; health is a blessing

33 BIO-ELEMENTS FOR AN ACTIVE HALAL LIFESTYLE

90
tablets

MADE IN UK   HALAL CERTIFIED

THE BOX OF MACAROONS

Provoking reactions is an integral part of what you do as a designer. To achieve that through your work, you have to bring in other elements to a project, mixing up the dynamics right from the start.

Some people like to work solely within a specific sector or style, for consistency or perhaps due to a thorough knowledge of a particular market segment. But I believe in the constant crossover, regularly taking on vastly different kinds of projects that in some way go on to influence one another. When you bring disparate elements to places they're least expected, they really stand out and surprise people. It's those moments that create conversation and excitement, and make people realise they can achieve more.

Before I do any design work for any new clients, I go through a stage of working on art direction and design strategy. I pull in lots of relevant reference images that help me explain my ideas, aiming high and showing amazing work from other people to set an ambitious benchmark.

Foil stamping references, colours, illustrations, paper samples, texture and all kinds of other ideas are often shown: but among my favourites to often put into a deck is a really vibrant, vivid box of macaroons. That array of punchy flavours coated in delicate colours screams bold, yet elegant.

While macaroons may seem erroneous to a branding project, that image needed to be in the deck to show positive energy – the ambition to be exciting again.

That slide always got a reaction: I wanted to show the client that they can look outside of the norm to build something new.

Client
Nathalie Gordon

Type
**Branding
+ Design**

NathalieGordon
PHOTOGRAPHY

nathaliegordon.com
310.866.3569

beauty **fashion** & PORTRAITS

MAKING THINGS HAPPEN ON THE GO

It goes without saying that our phones are no longer just for making calls – in fact, they're rarely used for talking, and frequently employed for documenting dinners, peeking into the world of others through Instagram stories or adorning our faces with bunny ears.

We have these powerful mini-computers sat in our pockets that are meant to be changing our lives for better, at least according to those who make them. Often, though, they're doing the opposite: sucking us in and surreptitiously stealing hours that could be used to make something exciting happen. We're all guilty of phone-induced time-wasting, so I often remind myself of the long-term value I can get out of every minute, and how devices can actually assist that.

As my phone is with me 24/7, I've learned how to use it to benefit me in starting new projects. A lot of ideas recorded on even basic phone apps have gone on to grow into much bigger projects.

For instance, I hadn't envisaged that recording local folklore in Uganda would result in a full audio-visual project, later released as an EP and music video. A drawing created on my phone became a sculpture. I've amended a client's brand guidelines using colour samples taken from physical, real-world materials captured on the go. Some of the Adobe Creative Cloud mobile apps have been fantastic for such processes. For example, Adobe Capture CC turns my photos into production-ready colour themes in just a few taps. A phone can be a scrapbook, notebook and aide memoir: you can make big plans on a small device and rest assured they're stored in the Cloud.

Despite dreams that I'd write the first Book of Ideas in an idyllic remote village, living out the bohemian lifestyle we imagine authors enjoy, the reality was rather different. It was mostly written on the go: commuting, between meetings, in taxis and so on. For all their negatives, phones can be a crucial assistant, there to record any flash of inspiration that might otherwise be quickly forgotten.

Client
Mystery Box

Type
Logo design

Client
StageStruck

Type
**Brand refresh
+ Design**

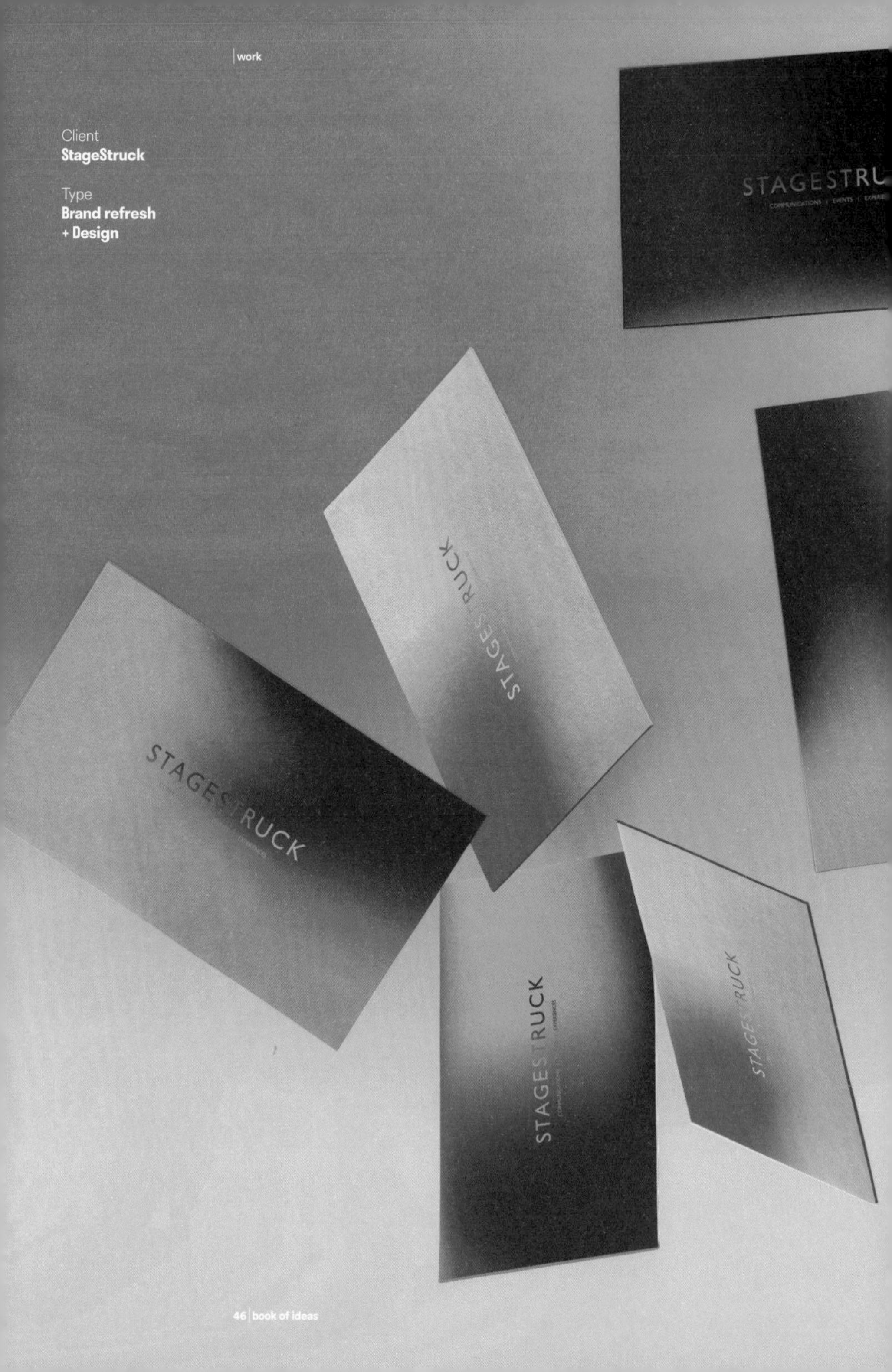

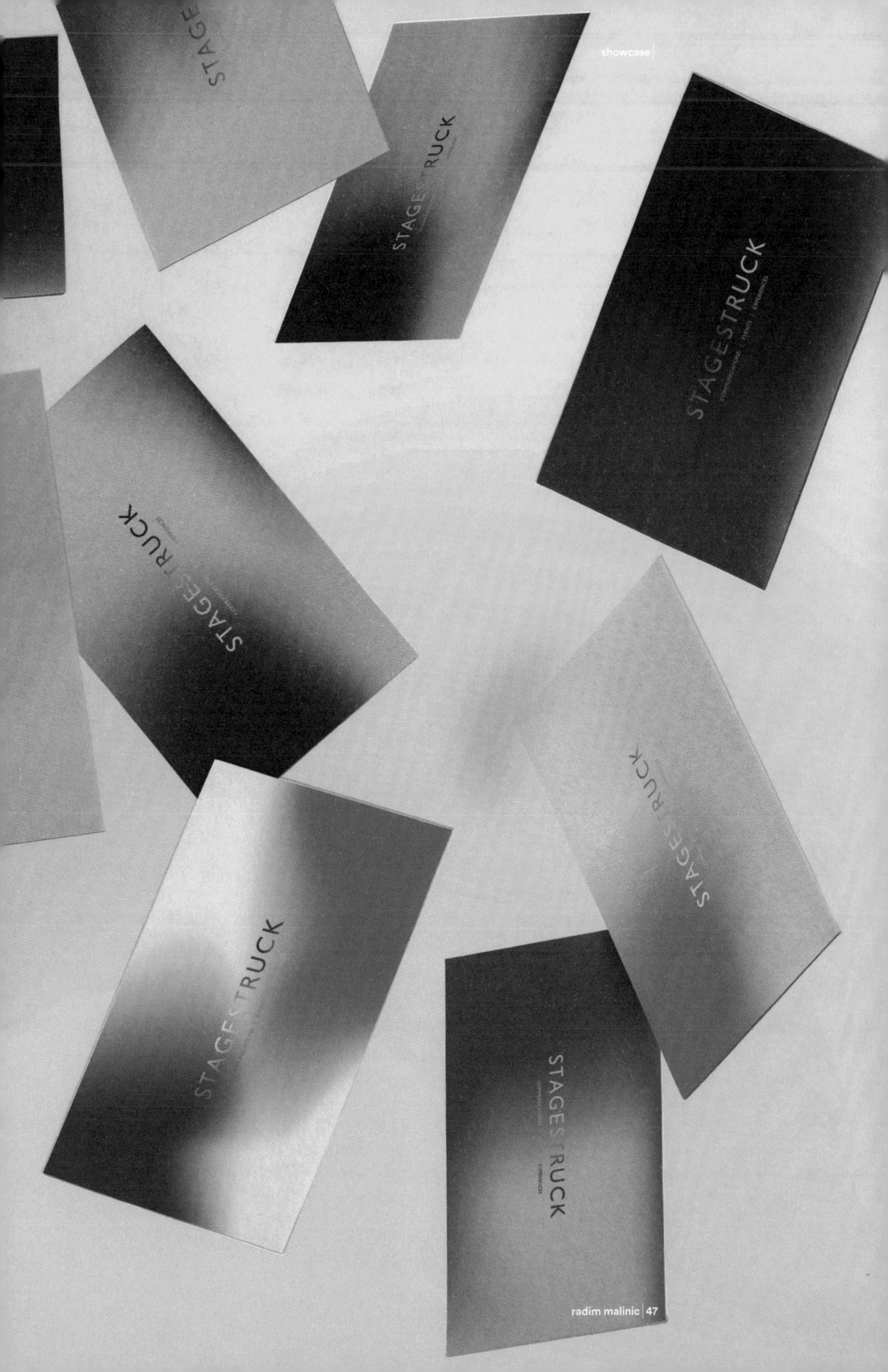
STAGESTRUCK
COMMUNICATIONS | EVENTS | EXPERIENCES

DREAM CLIENTS

There are two ways to define a "dream client".

For some designers or agencies, it might be one of a list of high-net-worth brands and companies they'd give an arm and a leg to work for. Another set of "dream" clients is defined as those you as a designer feel a true connection with: they might be an existing client or a new one, but ultimately they get where you're coming from and trust you fully to create the right work for the project.

The dream client for me is more the latter than the former.

Not all bucket list-type companies will be a dream to work with, and not all clients you feel a connection with will go on to remain dream-like for the entire duration of a project. Forming great client relationships takes time and effort on the designer's part as much as the client's, and it's up to both sides to use their skills and knowledge to turn something average into something great.

Maybe you know your dream clients already: you've made their impossible a reality time and time again. Those people have come to see your unrivalled passion and verve, and your ambitious drive to deliver their vision. Dream clients are the ones that unlock your confidence, helping you make their dreams come true.

As designers, we must take the time to understand and explain the options to those we're working with regarding what's expected of us, and how far we can deliver over and above what we were initially briefed to do. While you can't always ensure you work with dream clients, over time you can become a dream creative or agency. Experience teaches us how to become indispensable.

#weownthenight

birgerjarl

we are summer

twentyeighteen

Äntligen börjar våren och värmen ta fart och lika
så suget för fest. Lördagarna på bj är som alltid
överhettad med dans, kärlek och snygga gäster
oavsett om det är löning eller veckan före.

bj

birgerjarl.nu

#birgerjarl2018

info@birgerjarl.nu

NEDRE SLOTTSGATAN
753 09 UPPSALA

RESTAURANG & BAR
FRE - LÖR FRÅN 22:30

FRE TILL 03:00 (20 ÅR)
LÖR TILL 03:00 (23 ÅR)

STOP/START PRODUCTIVITY

I've been in the creative industries for about 15 years now, and in that time I've witnessed a huge shift in my own work. Mainly, the change has been in the time it takes to complete a project.

For the first few years, each new project would be finished within a few hours. Whether it was a poster or flyer design, 12" vinyl release or even a complex piece of digital illustration, the project would be done in less than one day.

In the next few years of my career, I was just as speedy and proficient with the software I use, but it would take a few days to complete a commission. I would slow down, take time away from the computer screen and really reflect on what I was doing. Today, a project now takes up to a few weeks to complete; with the design graft itself maybe taking six days or so. Now, I've realised the design work is only about a quarter of the process: the value comes from the time spent thinking, planning, sketching, validating and generally digesting the brief and what it requires. That's what forms the building blocks – the crucial, but often invisible underpinnings of the whole thing.

Complex tasks and projects are impossible to get right in one clean sweep. It's doable, of course: anything can be done quickly when your clients want to throw all their energy and resources at a last minute deadline. The results might work well, but they'll likely only do so for a short time. A good, holistic design project takes time with breaks to step away to get perspective and to recognise if it's truly good and has a potential to stands the test of time.

Stopping and starting can feel disrupting and irritating, especially if you've just started to really get into it. I used to hate leaving my desk even when I was "in the zone", chipping away. But I've learned to embrace the importance of wrenching myself away. In those situations, every time I came back to my work I would feel refreshed, with new angles and ideas on how to improve it.

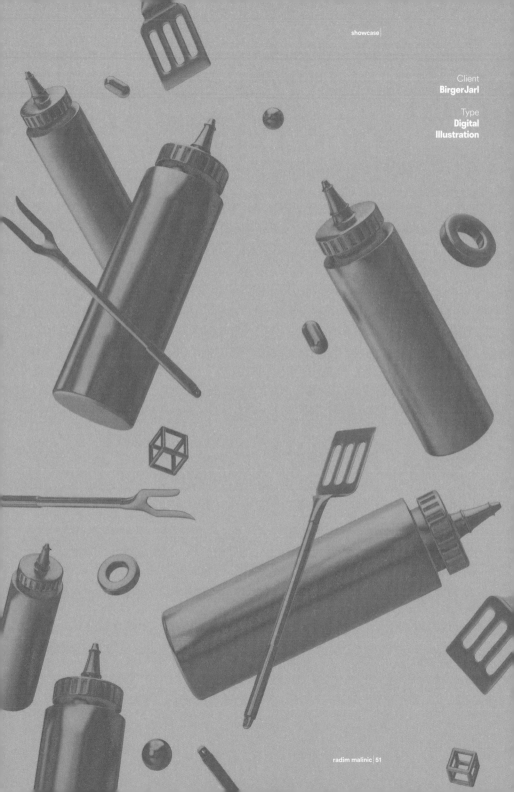

Client
BirgerJarl

Type
**Digital
Illustration**

THE PROBLEM WITH 'YESTERDAY'

When I first went freelance, my work was a mixture of direct client projects and commissions from other creative agencies. Often, that meant I had a deadline for every day of the week: I wanted to make an impression, and prove I was efficient and dependable. Obviously, working that way and promising crazy turnaround times was far from sustainable.

It felt like most of the external agency commissions had deadlines hovering around the "yesterday" mark. I often wondered why people worked that way, panicking at the last minute, then getting a freelancer in to plug a hole. That sort of work is relentless: you can work all night on revisions to find out in the morning that something's "not quite right", and you're back to square one. Some agencies abuse the power they have over newer designers, illustrators or art directors who are (initially) grateful for the gig.

After long years of nonsensical deadlines, I had to reflect on time planning – making work and life coexist more constructively. My creative practice now focuses on work for direct clients, some of whom I've worked with for many years. What's vital is allowing enough time for each and every project: there's no need to churn out half-baked work – you might make it quickly, but it won't stand the test of time.

Quality takes patience and reflection.

Nothing beats an honest conversation with your client and realistic planning. Create a sensible, manageable timeline and keep the client updated every step of the way. They'll love the fact they don't have to chase; you'll be remembered for transparency and clarity in what you deliver and how you deliver it. And crucially, you're in charge of your own time: no more "we need it yesterday" bullshit.

ÖPPETIDER
Fredagar 22.30-03.00
Lördagar 22.30- 03.00

HERE
COMES
SUMMER

birgerjarl

SOMMAR

twentysixteen

SOMMARENS
BÄSTA
NOJE

CONTACT
T 018-13 50 00
F 018-13 00 12

BIRGERJARL
Nedre Slottsgatan 3
753 09 Uppsala

16

WE OWN
THE NIGHT

SOMMAREN PÅ BIRGERJARL

BIRGERJARL.NU

ÖPPETIDER
Fredagar 22.30 -03.00
Lördagar 22.30- 03.00

VINTER PÅ BIRGERJARL

BIRGERJARL.NU

birgerjarl

16

WE OWN
THE NIGHT

CONTACT
T 018-13 50 00
F 018-13 00 12

BIRGERJARL
Nedre Slottsgatan 3
753 09 Uppsala

VISUAL STORYTELLING

Client
Computer Arts

Type
**Editorial
illustration**

In collaboration with
Tamas Arpadi

Art direction
Mark Wynne

Clients love to pick images from your showcase pieces,
looking to closely recreate that original work despite the fact
they're setting a completely different brief. It can be a strange
situation – you feel humbled you made the cut, but you only did
so to follow an existing style and template. Sometimes you find
little wiggle room to go beyond a signature style, or a client's
wishes to emulate references found online or elsewhere.

It's great to catch someone's attention with one of your favourite
pieces of work, but the next obstacle is to challenge the brief
itself and see how much further it could be pushed to turn it into
something original. This editorial project stemmed from a piece
of event advertising I created: it acted as a base idea, but
I made sure it wasn't simply to be repeated.

Editorial design and illustration can be some of the most enjoyable
work going because the work is based on elements and stories
that create a broader narrative and allow us to put a new spin
on visually representing a text.

To keep each element playing an equal part in this story, this image
for Computer Arts was created in Cinema 4D with five different
spot illustrations to get the balance right. A tricky tradeoff between
elegance and meaning had to be achieved.

If you look closely, there's an abstract letterform in each image,
too. Only when we knew we had each setting working and telling
its story without extra clutter, the final piece was assembled
into the page layout.

The Computer Arts art editor was supplied with five more images
than he expected, bringing an extra headache – he decided
to redesign the whole article to accommodate the spot pieces
more prominently. It's always nice to give people extras, and
occasionally, the "good" type of a headache.

Client
Computer Arts

Image
**Editorial
Illustration**

Client
Computer Arts

Image
Book Publishing

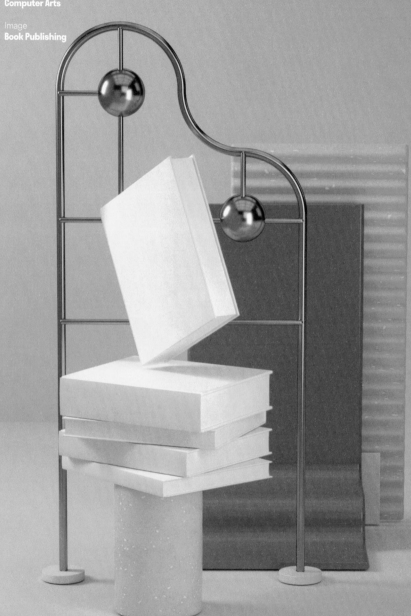

Client
Computer Arts

Image
Online Teaching

Client
Computer Arts

Image
Selling Merchandise

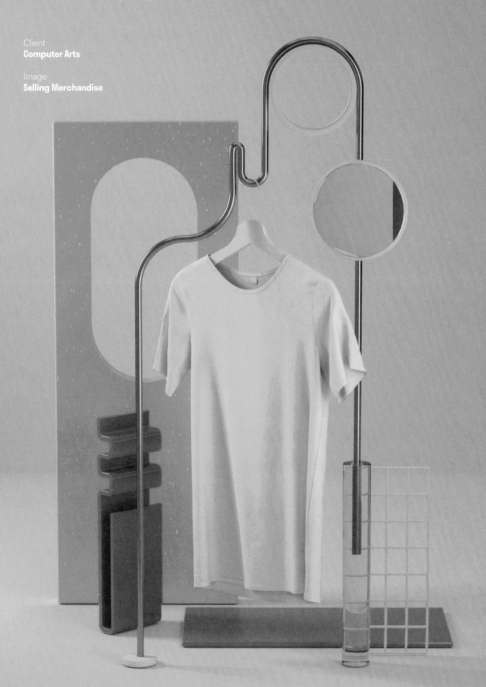

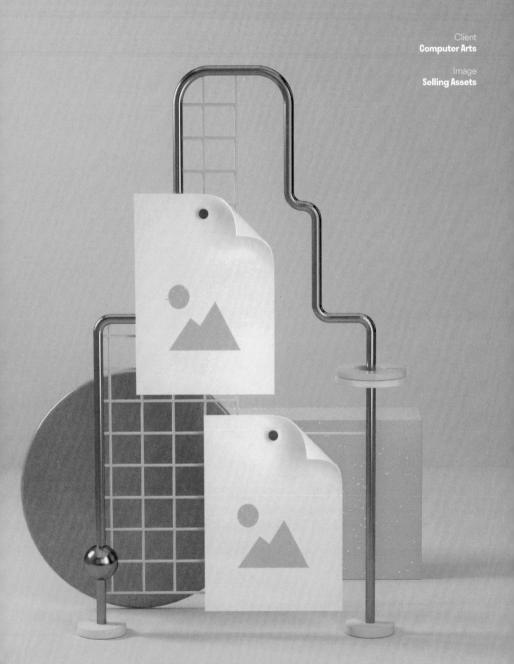

Client
Computer Arts

Image
Selling Assets

DESIGNING FOR SEASONS

Client
Birger Jarl

Type
Event Branding

In collaboration with
Tamas Arpadi

This a story of two halves. The collaboration with Swedish nightclub Birger Jarl started enthusiastically, took a turn for the worse, and emerged as one of the most enjoyable projects I've worked on.

A few years into the collaboration, I felt we didn't understand each other and some of the work felt really hard to get over the line despite its colourful and playful nature. I was planning to quit the project, only to be convinced by my partner to keep going. I'm glad she was there to talk sense into me. From that point onwards, things have gone from strength to strength. I no longer ponder what they might want – instead, I made it my priority to change the process. First, I send an art direction pitch to explain my ideas. Only then do we head into the design and focus on the outcome. I've worked for Birger Jarl twice a year for a decade now. They are my dream client and I make sure they know it every single time.

There's never a set client brief – in fact, there's never any brief. To keep our collaboration strong, we start afresh every time: that means we always start with a clean state, and that there isn't an option to take the easy route, however tempting it might be to carry something forward that worked well before.

Choosing from 20 completed campaigns was never going to be easy, but the Fifteen Year Anniversary work deserved a spotlight. The visuals were based on the idea of how each previous year was different to the one before. The key visual, 'No.15', was designed as a flat vector in Adobe Illustrator in various colourways to establish the palette. The parts of the 3D lettering pieces were set within a space to merge together on the reveal – this was key for the animation, where abstract shapes meet at the end to form the shape and meaning.

The various camera angles gave us options to use the more abstract pieces as teaser posters before the main campaign was revealed. They added extra depth and a hint of intrigue to the project. The option to keep pushing ahead with fresh concepts means there's less worrying about surpassing the previous work: when we purely focus on the work itself, we can enjoy what we do and keep growing.

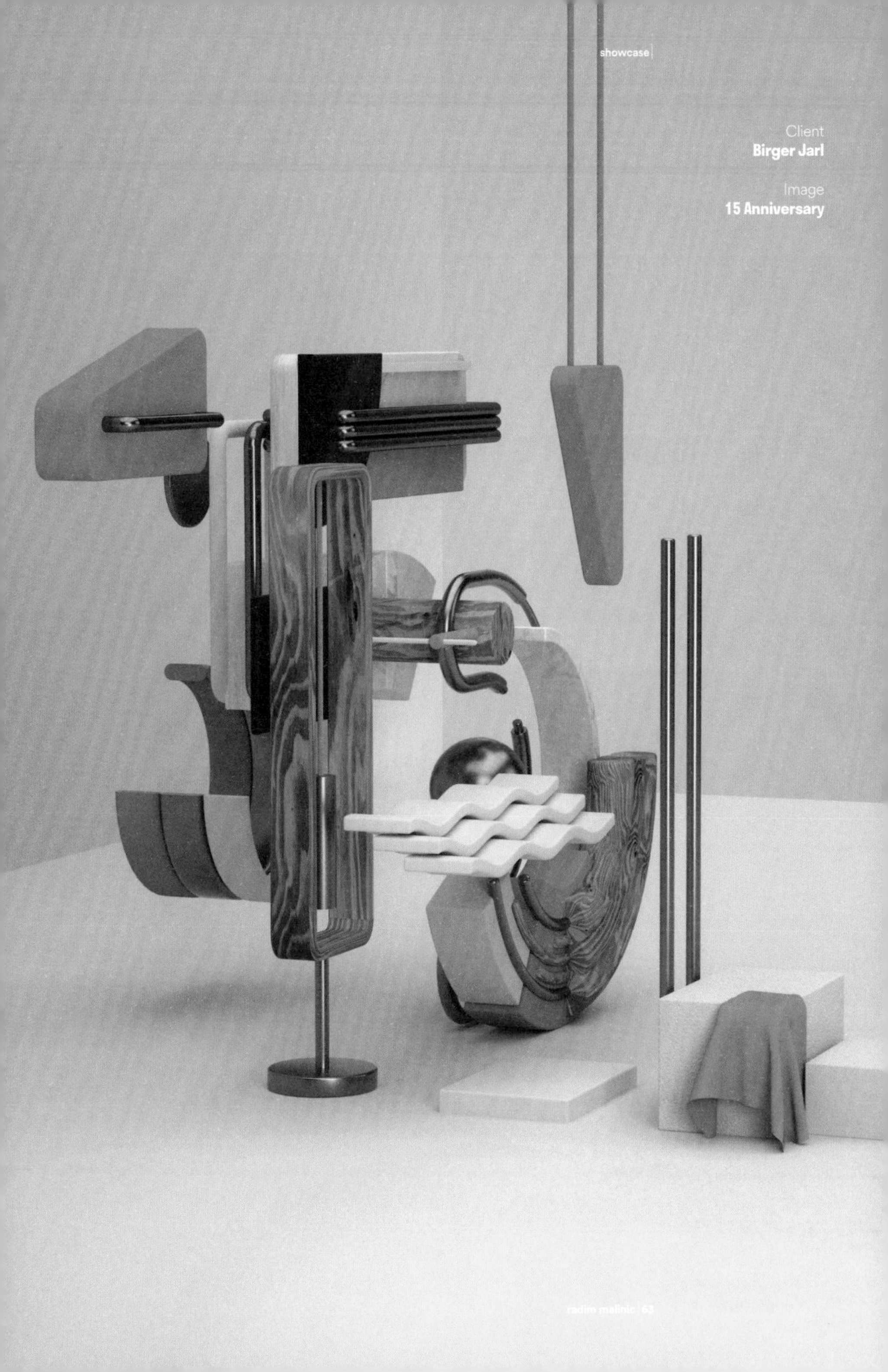

Client
Birger Jarl

Image
15 Anniversary

Client
Birger Jarl

Image
Typography

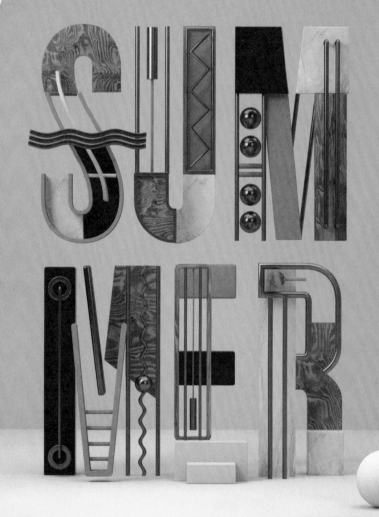

Client
Birger Jarl

Image
Poster Design

birgerjarl

Tiden går fort när man har roligt. I är fyller Birgerjarl fantastiska 15 år som nöjesmetropol i Uppsala.

2002 —

FIFTEEN

Tiden går fort när man har roligt. I är fyller Birgerjarl fantastiska 15 år som nöjesmetropol i Uppsala. Helg efter helg har vi levererat galna där gästerna kommit från världens alla hörn. Vi kör därför en stor jubileumsfest lördag 1/7 med artister, djs och roliga.

WE ARE

Nedre Slottsgatan 3
753 09 Uppsala

T 018-13 50 00
F 018-13 00 12

birgerjarl.nu

#weownthenight

Tiden går fort när man har roligt.
I är fyller Birgerjarl fantastiska 15 år.

2017 —

Client
Birger Jarl

Type
**Bottle
Graphics**

Client
Birger Jarl

Image
Poster Design

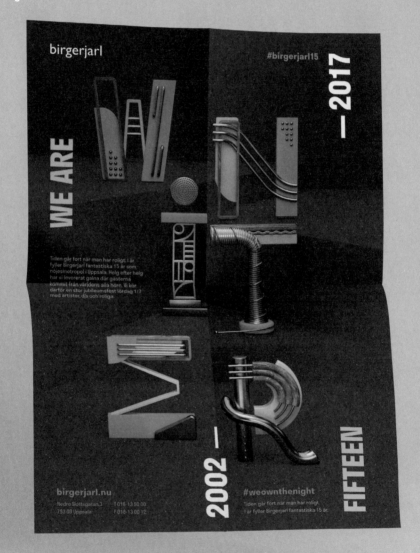

Client
Birger Jarl

Image
Typography

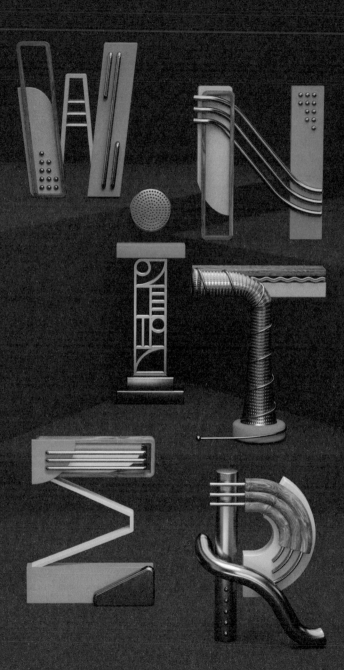

FOOD FOR THOUGHT

Client
Better:You

Type
**Branding + Design
+ Illustration**

In collaboration with
Craig Minchington

The world of fitness, wellbeing and nutrition is full of predictable images. The plan for the Better:You brand refresh was to re-engineer the wheel. Each illustration aimed to portray the various disciplines that make up the business: nutritional therapy, personal training, weight loss, consultation and even cooking lessons.

The modelling was made with white clay models and no colour. The CGI artist, Bristol-based Craig Minchington, was given only a list of objects I wanted to include – we didn't waste any energy writing long-winded emails, instead we chatted on the phone and Skype about potential ideas that could help us succeed. Making changes on the fly with screen share simulated sharing the same office space environment, even though everyone working on the project was hundreds of miles apart.

Usually, my creative work uses multiple shades of numerous colours, but here, we needed to drastically cut down the choices. We did colour tests with a shade of navy blue and highlights in gold: it soon became clear no other colours were needed.

One element of the system made many people smile: the blue avocado with a gold stone in the middle. We enjoyed quite a few funny comments on social media. For that reason, I decided to commission a resin sculpture designer to make three of these avocados for real. I failed to mention what size I envisaged them, and it turns out that where the maker lives in Scotland, the avocados are pretty huge.

Behance picked up this project when it launched as one of the trendsetting pieces for the year ahead. Of course, we didn't necessarily intend to set a trend with this work, we just wanted it to be as strong as possible. We wanted to have fun with it and make it work for the business. The rest was an added bonus.

The impact of ownable branding assets can never be underestimated: the effort and resources devoted to creating them always reaps rewards.

Client
Better:You

Image
App screen

Client
Better:You

Image
About Us

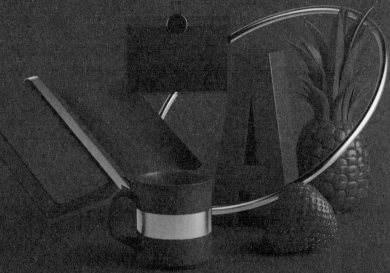

Client
Better:You

Image
**Nutritional
Therapy**

Client
Better:You

Image
**Resin sculpture
by Chris Alexander**

Client
Better:You

Image
**Personal
Training**

Client
Better:You

Image
**Cooking
Classes**

OPPOSITES ATTRACT

Client
Mutual Attraction

Type
**Branding + Design
+ Illustration**

In collaboration with
Craig Minchington

After our initial art direction strategy meeting for matchmaking agency Mutual Attraction, I knew the new branding system aimed to be elegant, fairly minimal and sophisticated.

I started searching for the big idea. We asked: "What does attraction look like? How do you visually represent that ineffable chemistry that makes us fall in love with each other?" It made me think about the different shapes, sizes and colours we all come in; about our different ideas and interests. "Opposites attract" became the overarching idea, and every design decision was based on it.

The red and blue opposing sides of a magnet inspired the contrasts that makeup Mutual Attraction's typographic logo. I then looked for other visual references to form the broader system, and the colour wheel provided many contrasting options until we settled on pink and green. Serif and sans serif fonts were used for the very same reason – their contrast – so there was no need to test the logo in 20 different styles, we had the logic right there. All collateral, such as business cards and stationery, was based on the opposites attract theme too, with information placed in opposite corners or on different sides of the canvas.

We wanted to showcase the real people who found love through Mutual Attraction, who would be a perfect testimony to the company's services. Well, that was the plan until we ran out of budget for a photo shoot. So I decided to spend the rest of the available budget on 3D design. We created eight images based on a narrative of dating, and got to work on a set of isometric illustrations that portray everything from looking for love to coffee dates, movie nights and city breaks, to moving in together and getting married. The brand colour rules that were set at the beginning made the process easier, as the emphasis was put on one object in colour contrast.

As soon as the images were implemented across the print and digital touchpoints, the whole system felt complete. The move to use a drastically different approach to the rest of the industry paid off, seeing increased brand awareness and trust, as well as new clients.

Client
Mutual Attraction

Image
Movie Date

Client
Mutual Attraction

Image
Logo Design

mutual | ATTRACTION

Client
Mutual Attraction

Image
Business Cards

Client
Mutual Attraction

Image
Looking for love

Client
Mutual Attraction

Image
Coffee Date

Client
Mutual Attraction

Image
City Break

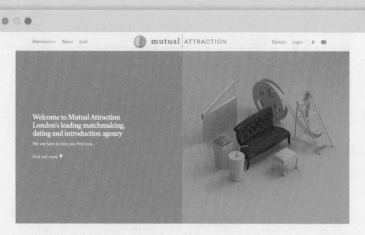

Membership About Live!   mutual | ATTRACTION   Contact Login

Welcome to Mutual Attraction
London's leading matchmaking,
dating and introduction agency

We are here to help you find love...

Find out more ▼

About   Meet the Team

Mutual Attraction is a London dating agency and matchmaking service.

welcome

We are so glad you found us!

We are a team of London matchmakers who get people serious about love, into serious relationships.

If you're a happy, successful and interesting Londoner living life to the full, and are looking for someone amazing to share it with, then you my friend, are in the right place.

Let us let you in on a secret.

The good guys and the incredible women haven't all been 'snapped up'. Far from it.

How do we know? Because we work with them!

we are an award winning London dating agency

We know you're probably feeling a bit jaded with dating which is why we'll do all the hard work for you. We'll get to know you, meet people on your behalf and then introduce you to your matches.

We're offline, confidential and discreet. Our clients expect no less. We are a slice of luxury love in a world of tinder hookups.

Membership   How does it work

Looking for a lasting, loving and committed relationship?

Click here to start your journey and become a member

We believe everyone deserves a loving and happy relationship.

Finding your life partner is one of the biggest decisions you will ever make, so why leave it to chance?

MAKING DATA LOOK GREAT

Client
Harnham

Type
**Branding + Design
+ Illustration + Web**

In collaboration with
Tamas Arpadi

I was in the boardroom with data and analytics recruitment company Harnham to hear a discussion about its existing brand, and that it really wasn't working. I made sure I only spelt out the implications of using the old identity going forward, not just shooting it to pieces. 'So how much for a couple of logo ideas?' was the dreaded question. 'A million pounds,' I joked. There's no chance you can nail a logo brief without having any prior knowledge of who you're working for. It turned out that someone only a few weeks prior delivered 18 – yes, 18 –logo concepts that didn't make the cut.

This project exemplifies how the "funnel of output" came to exist in my working practice. It was the first instance where I put full emphasis on pre-design planning and research. The time piecing image references together and forming a clear, concise path proved crucial. We had two meetings where I presented 50-page PDFs proposing a direction and vision.

Through lengthy conversations and we agreed on an art direction strategy. Now almost seven years later, the results of those conversations are still very much integral to the whole design system. I came to pitch one logo concept on the back of the research, then watched the board of directors look a bit puzzled until about the fifteenth slide where the proposal came together. It clicked for everyone: all the work that followed began from that point, and the output multiplied exponentially. Single-colour branding expanded to using different colour palettes for each part of the business, and a full custom icon system was drawn.

We progressed the simple, two-dimensional illustrations into the world of 3D design, adding more depth and meaning. We created a design system that enabled multiple layers building from the original idea, meaning the brand can constantly evolve with elegance and authority.

All our choices were always going be very bold given the nature of the competition: the data and analytics recruitment market isn't known for forward-thinking graphic design.

Client
Harnham

Image
Digital Analytics

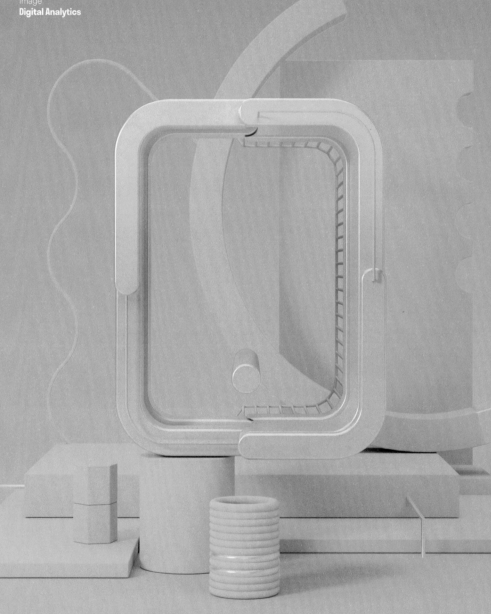

Client
Harnham

Image
Salary Guide

Project
harnham.com - website design

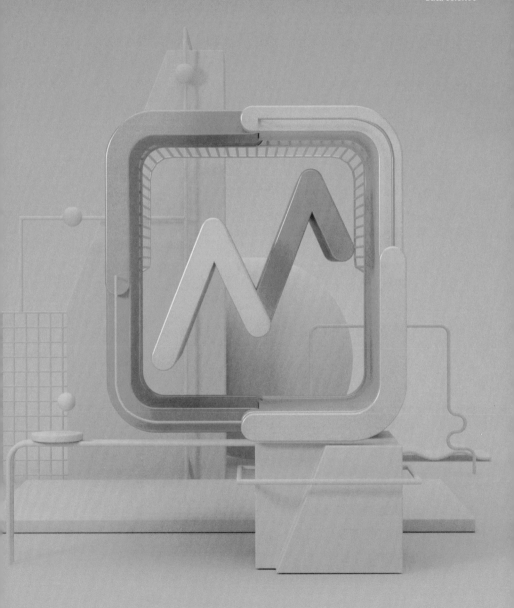

Client
Harnham

Image
**Salary Guide
cover**

CREATIVITY

Everyone has the power to change the world in some small way.

The **Creativity** section touches on how to build career paths by making conscious choices around who to work with; how to decode our own creative DNA; the ingredients that inform our decisions; the weight of the imagination; using humour; how to entertain the "right wrongs" and improving our work through more skilful use of language.

AMBITION v REALITY

How did you feel on your first day at a new job? Apprehensive?
Excited? Confident? Or did you feel like an impostor? I remember
how proud I was to take on the title of "graphic designer" right from
day one. I actually felt the opposite of impostor syndrome: I was
so excited that I didn't have time to dwell on my blissful ignorance.
I felt like an invincible designing machine, ready to solve all the
world's creative needs despite being in the job less than a fortnight
and having never produced any proper client work in my role. That
excitement gave me a false sense of security – I was armed with
heaps of ambition and none of the necessary doubt. I thought
I knew I what it took to turn the visions in my head into a reality.
But when I look back into what I used to produce, ambition and
reality didn't match. Sometimes not even in the slightest.

I was blindly willing to fight over simple stuff with the client where
I was clearly in the wrong. I was being a fool – and worst of all,
I wasn't even aware I was. As time passed and my willingness to
fight receded, I began to achieve some sort of balance and less
desire to always dominate the process.

We need to be the client's best friend, guide, concierge, confidant
and trusted buddy to enable the best working setup possible.
While all of that won't be always possible, human interaction is one
the most vital ingredients in a successful creative process. Nothing
beats the moment when you click with a prospective client from
the first handshake. It feels like a half of the project is won already.

You are the face of your business, and your work is the face of your
creativity. Make sure people can see both from the outset. No one
likes an asshole. The day you take on a fancy new job title is the day
when the journey begins. It might take a while until you ambitions
start resembling the reality.

Many years later, I feel I'm getting closer to turning my ambitions
into reality; and part of that is realising I am still very much at
the beginning.

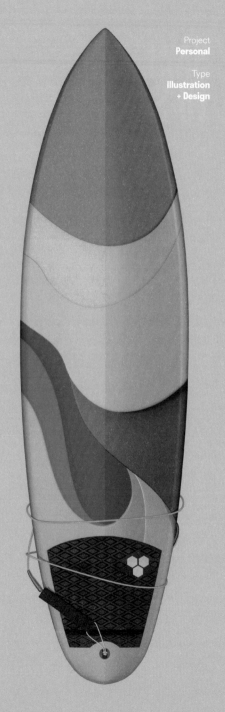

SAY LITTLE TO SAY A LOT

I was once on the phone to an art editor discussing the illustration I was producing for their magazine. I'd spent hours making sure my piece had depth and detail – it was already quite complex. Glad to learn he was happy with my work, I was expecting it to be signed off right there and then. To my surprise, he concluded, "keep going, add more layers". Looking back, this was somewhat my own fault: I used to overload pretty much every illustration. I spent hours and hours adding more detail and extras, believing I was doing the right thing.

Over time, those numerous layers and details became my style, until I realised I had nothing more to add. I started to go the other way. Gradually, I started to ask myself how I can tell the same visual story but with fewer elements.

I started heading back to where I once was – the simple and balanced space where I felt a lot more comfortable.

Everyone is guilty of over-complicating everything in their life sometimes, especially when we feel exposed and yearn for approval. We dive into endless revisions to make ourselves believe that adding extras is the solution. It's the opposite.

The beauty of a big idea is in the purity of its narrative. Impact comes from cutting the confusing side plots that don't support your story.

You need practice to fully understand your tools: no songwriter writes a pop song by chance, nor do they write it the first time they pick up an instrument. They write it after years of honing their craft. They learn the scales back to front and understand the logic. Then, they might write the simple three-chord wonder with the right arrangement that will set the world alight.

Client
Birger Jarl

Type
**Running club
top design**

FIND (AND BE) A MENTOR

Even when you've been around the block a few times and passed certain career milestones, it can be incredibly helpful to take a moment to get an outside view of your world. For better or worse, I never had a mentor in my design career. I had to work out many career and business decisions without any fallback.

I made a ton of bad decisions without knowing what I was getting myself into. But I got through it all.

If you're like me – the worst mixture of stubborn, passionate and determined – then it's wise to check in with someone to see if you're doing the right thing. Even though you might be right on the cusp of something new and significant, you should still ask for a second opinion.

I love people of the same persuasion – the bloody-minded ones focused on making something out of their time on the planet. I always have time for young designers, art students or anyone who gets in touch with curious questions on how to get ahead. I love that raw energy and intent.

Now as a mentor, I've been learning empathy and understanding, and I'm beginning to navigate how to instigate a logical structure into working life, which is something I am still trying to master myself. Listening to and helping others has, in turn, helped me to refocus my work and career. The process is beneficial for both parties.

It's never too late to find a mentor, so don't be shy.

We're all only human. Sooner or later you'll repay the gift by mentoring someone else.

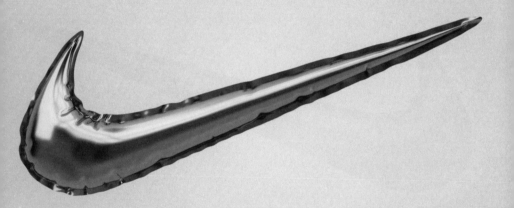

Project
Air Max Day 2018

Type
Illustration

Project
Air Max Day 2018

Type
Illustration

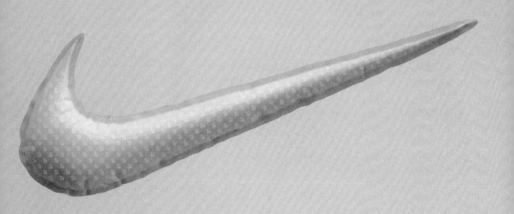

AN INFLUENTIAL COMMUNITY

Have a think about those people in your circle of friends or colleagues who inspire you the most. To smash an industry myth, you don't need to live in the middle of a creative metropolis to have a chance at building an illustrious long-term career. These days, it doesn't matter where you are, there will always be an opportunity waiting for you somewhere.

I built the foundations of my creative career from a spare bedroom in a small town on the south coast of England. Thanks to the internet, of course, I could share my work with everyone in the world. This was also very much a pre-social media era, and before the time people worked in cafes and co-working spaces, but I was in touch with countless fellow designers and illustrators who were in the exact same position, scattered around the globe.

Even though we may have appeared less "connected" in the early 2000s, the truth was the opposite. I remember having a few hundred contacts in my instant messenger application for daily exchanges of tips, ideas and collaborations. It felt like a truly magical time and I stay in touch with most of those creatives today. It feels like we graduated from the same university at the same time, even though everyone lives on different continents and some of us never even met. The key to our community was the desire to stay in touch and share the ups and downs of our daily escapades, learning from one another.

Hearing experiences from different places was inspiring and refreshing, and the hunger and passion of like-minded souls were motivating. Your influential community goes way beyond the connect, follow or add friend buttons on social media sites.

It's important to build your own influential circle of friends, but you have to make a conscious decision to do so and maintain it. Contact your design idol or dream collaborator; shake hands with a keynote speaker, or simply ping an email to someone whose work you appreciate: that could be the start of a regular conversation that will enrich your creative life. While some people have egos the size of Manhattan, there are far more great people who are willing to share their life lessons with you.

Project
Ciclo Retro

Type
**Cycling jersey
design**

EXPLORE YOUR SILLY

I've chalked up a long list of mishaps and daft endeavours in my time, taking in both intentional and accidental fuck ups. I like to have fun and I explore my silly side a lot – I try to find a joke in everything. Unless the joke finds me.

One Saturday summer evening in London, I was heading home on an overground train that bore the stench of a kebab shop. To my disbelief, there was no one else in the carriage: that ravenous army must have alighted just before I got on. Of course, I followed the social media protocol and posted a tweet joking about the situation. I watched amused replies coming thick and fast.

Spurred on by those Twitter replies, by using stock images I made a Photoshop mockup of a luxurious London Overground Takeaway fragrance set, stretching a silly idea to breaking point and, of course, sharing it online again. It made me smile and I was going to leave it there. But it turned out it made a few prospective clients smile: the joke project worked as a conversation starter that made discussing new projects less corporate and lots more friendly.

Design, branding and advertising are using a lot less humour than I can remember, and both sides of the equation are to blame. As customers we want our products and services to be delivered by professionals who take their craft seriously; and as designers, we want to make work that will last, nothing too needy or hipsterish. But maybe we're all taking ourselves a little too seriously: perhaps it's time to lighten up a bit sometimes and bring the fun back into our work.

Like most, my creative practice isn't based on humour-filled projects: I take on a broad spectrum of work that requires building trust with clients and customers. That's why I explore my silly when possible, using such time as a muscle-flexing exercise to counterbalance the conference calls, invoice-chasing and meetings about meetings. Whether it's a quick digital doodle, pencil sketch, Tweet or diary entry, I urge you to make people smile once in a while with stuff you create. It turns out that silly work can lead to bigger things. A fun approach can make you happier, and your work better.

AUTHENTIC
SATURDAY NIGHT
SCENT

KEBAB
+CHIPS

IN A PUDDLE
OF MAYO

EAU DE TRAIN CARRIAGE
6.7 FL. OZ / 200ML

GALLERY vs HIGH STREET

The serene experience of a silent, high-ceilinged museum or white-walled gallery can feel like an escapist tonic to our relentlessly connected digital lives. It's so important to take a moment to really observe the work of your favourite practitioners, poring over their brushwork and craft details.

In the lifetime of a commercial creative, the majority of the work produced is destined for mainstream crowd consumption. Regardless of the client or commission size, what we do on a day-to-day basis isn't always here for the long haul. It isn't museum fodder.

Contemporary creativity can feel quite far removed from the classics. The advent of fast fashion and throwaway culture gives a sense that our material possessions have very limited value soon after their purchase. The next big thing is already happening, if it didn't happen yesterday.

As those who play their part in the infinite consumption cycle – us in the creative industries – we have to keep abreast of the developments that are happening on the high street. You have to be in touch with the people buying the stuff we make, all the while studying the old, observing the now and inventing the new of the future.

Studying the high street is as important as time spent in a design museum: you have to see creativity in use first hand, in the "real world". If only one piece of our work ended up in a museum collection, we would feel extremely proud. But work is rarely created for a museum: it earned its right to be there.

We need influences from across the spectrum of high art to high street. Only when we have an understanding of the world around us, and where our work goes, do we have a chance to combine beautiful work with functional design.

Client
Farske

Type
**Branding
+ Packaging**

Project
Lowe Clothing

Type
Logo design

In collaboration with
Anna Mullin

EST. 2018

LÖWE

ACTIVEWEAR

FINEST TAILORING & FINEST COTTON
MADE AROUND THE WORLD
DESIGNED IN LONDON

Project
Lowe Clothing

Type
**Bottle
graphics**

A CORRIANDER STORY

Few things have influenced why I got into the world of creativity as much as my mum's cooking. She made the simplest food look sumptuously beautiful: even her beans on toast could have earned a Michelin star.

That's one of the big reasons I give a damn about every detail of what I create. However simple the work, it's meant to make someone fall in love with it. I aim to emulate every single plate of my mum's food, apart from one "evil" ingredient: coriander. I couldn't get on with it for decades.

As humans, our palettes supposedly broaden after we turn 30. For me, coriander and country music were both in the same category. While I can ignore country music quite easily, I couldn't get to grips with coriander until well into my late 30s.

Sometimes the most memorable moments happen when we least expect them. I excitedly ordered a bowl of Poke food one sunny day in London. That joy waned when the coriander made an appearance, but as a Czech emigree, I've lived in the UK long enough to know to politely smile when internally freaking out. To my surprise, the food was phenomenal: it looked great and tasted even better. I was converted there and then.

Each of my clients has their own coriander. We all have something that bothers us, and that's ok. Nonetheless, it's simply astonishing to learn the ingredients behind why some of our creative choices aren't compatible to someone's taste. One of my career aims is to help people tackle their own coriander, and try everything.

We should be able to design things that can change people's mindsets. Variety is the key to long-term satisfaction. Beautiful food tastes better, regardless of how simple the recipe might be. Beautiful design that looks great and works even better can convert people too.

Client
Gerry's Diner

Type
**Branding
+ Design**

CRACKING YOUR CREATIVE DNA

How can we crack the code that informs our creative decisions?
We need to discover who we are, what drives our creativity forward and what hinders it. Numerous books endeavour to help us tackle how we come to creative decisions, but it can be broken into a simple equation:

Inspiration + influence + information = your creative DNA

Like most people, I didn't consider those three elements for a long time into my career, but it's a revelation to break them down to see how they shape our thinking, doing and making. It helps to inform and shape the future.

Inspiration - When a moment makes you feel something or a passing idea urges you to take action. While inspiration can be elusive, the key is to let it enter your life, but don't chase it. An open and curious mind is the one that finds the most fascinating pieces of future work. Colour inspires me no end – its meaning, history, theory, scientific use and reactions to it.

Influence - It's constantly around us and it shapes our life experiences, from the basic to profound. Every meaningful experience has an effect on us. Take a moment to understand the processes that make up everything around us, and they can give you a direction for your own work.

Information - Direction based on facts and reasoning. Even just scratching the surface of the vast swathes of information around us can be hugely beneficial. I might be inspired by colour, but I can only make better colour choices based on the science of colour. I love science, biology, psychology, anthropology, behavioural economics and many others – all of those play a key part in my creative decision-making.

Everyone should be encouraged to take time to decipher their own creative process and DNA. Only by looking into every detail can you use these findings to your favour for better and more meaningful work.

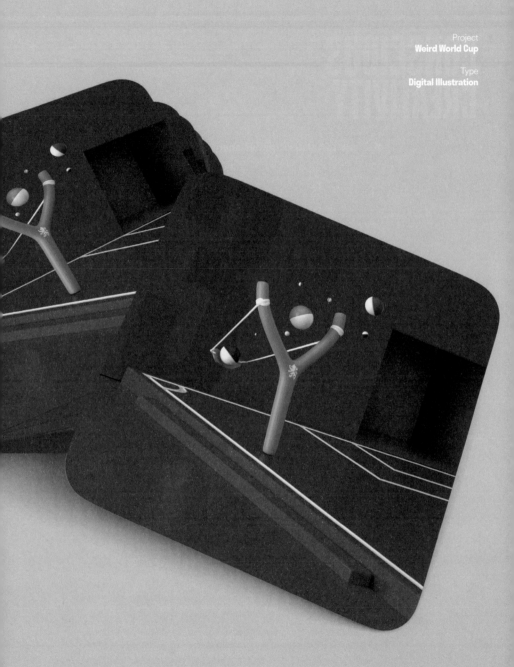

CONSCIOUS CREATIVITY

It's time to bolster creative energy towards making the world be a better place. Centuries of human life have made such a negative imprint on the globe, which future generations will have a very hard time rectifying. Without sounding like too much of a hippie, I believe every single person has the ability to influence the future of tomorrow.

I give a shit and I try to do something about it. So you can imagine the spring in my step when I was on my way to a meeting with a forward-thinking social impact start-up with a grand vision for their product. But while listening to their company values, I couldn't help notice that both of the directors consumed three small plastic bottles of water during the meeting. I left in disbelief.

Today's world resembles a groggy morning after a night on the tiles, feeling sick and remorseful and wondering how to fix it all. But the hair of the dog won't solve anything: escapism isn't a viable solution long term.

We're collectively culpable in ignoring the big issues in favour of our own little worlds, viewing our individual impact as insignificant. I now see my work as tools that I can use to work with those who have even greater visions to create products and services that benefit our future.

Fortune 500 brands are increasingly launching 'good cause' projects and (supposedly) trying to use their wealth to fix the world. While I still work with some of these multinational brands, I try to make sure it's part of a bigger initiative to ensure there's a balance – a 'good energy' footprint to offset the bad. I've turned down many commissions from oil companies, plastic producers, fake fur brands and so on because I didn't want to aid something I don't believe in. Of course, those types of projects are often the best paid.

There are many people out there who have fantastic innovation ideas that can make all of our futures better, so do your utmost to help them succeed through great creative work.

Project
Poison Flora

Type
Digital Illustration

Project
Poison Flora

Type
Notebook

Project
Poison Flora

Type
Digital Illustration

THE RIGHT WRONG

We all have the capacity to imagine the future, but we mostly catastrophise about what's to come with little evidence to back up our visions of doom. Let's say your favourite musician collaborates with a (terrible) pop star: we immediately assume it won't go well. But at least that news makes us feel something, and that's not always a bad thing.

Sometimes the best creative solutions arise from unexplored paths we might usually wince at. We should embrace being unsure, even when the alternative is more comfortable. Opportunities to entertain a notion that just doesn't sit right should be explored.

It can feel double scary to bring an unusual idea to life. If the "right wrong" idea doesn't stop bothering you for a long time, that's a strong argument for making it happen.

Of course, you can set up a network of friends who can make sure you're not committing straight-up career sabotage by putting work that's far too crazy for the world out there. Almost every musician is guilty of bringing out an odd album, authors experiment with different styles and techniques, forward-thinking architects try to reshape the world around us to make us feel something new.

Breaking the norm is more often than not a welcome addition to any creative oeuvre.

While the right right is too right and wrong wrong is just plain wrong, the right wrong is the best of both worlds. If it excites at least one person, then that's a reason to stop second-guessing yourself. Make your idea happen.

The right wrong can be a thing of a beauty.

Client
Lux Coffee Roasters

Type
Packaging

LEARNING TO FLY

I believe the true leaders are the ones that know their business inside out, as well as the people they lead. They know how to look out for people, they can spot an issue before it happens and find the right fix. Leaders like these have gone through the ranks, learning over the years to build their knowledge and skill set piece by piece.

A friend of mine landed a managerial job in one of the most respected restaurant groups in London. He'd been in the game for many years and was extremely good at what he did, but he knew he had extensive training ahead of him. He spent months working within different departments, everywhere from the kitchen to reservations to the front of the house. He got to meet and learn about every other employee and their role in the company's operations. He later became an operations manager and went on to successfully open many new restaurant sites for the group.

The rigorous and lengthy process he went through both improves skills and brings people together to work as a tight-knit group. People look out for each other. Many other restaurant groups have followed suit with such training.

Is it time to apply a process like that in creative agencies? Just imagine the face of a new creative director if he was being asked to sit with a team of junior designers for a couple of weeks. The best type of work happens through collaboration, and a mutual understanding of one another's skills and philosophies.

If only we had the time and financial resources to get every new manager, account handler or creative director familiarised with the inner runnings of an agency. Can you imagine the change of mood? Productivity and the work itself would improve, staff would likely stick around for longer and egos would bluster a lot less.

Project
November Universe

Type
**Product
development**

WHY vs HOW

"I love it. How did you make it? Can you post a tutorial?"
What software did you use?" Such comments are frequently
spotted below YouTube videos, Instagram posts and on any
other sharing platform, you care to name.

While they can be very encouraging for the creator, they can
also often give people the wrong idea. People see something that
seems new and want to have a go at using that "secret ingredient"
for themselves, right that second.

The questions about the "why" should also be about the "how".
People love to think that extremely imaginative work created
over months or even years can be distilled into a few step-by-step
guides to help them achieve the same results without
much effort, or knowing the actual reason it was created.

We live in the most creatively privileged times ever, a design
Disneyland of software-led possibilities. No longer do we
consider the hours, days, weeks and months that go into making
something great. We can achieve results in a fraction of the time
of our predecessors, so it's very tempting to think we can keep
shortening the time it takes to turn the blank page into something
extraordinary. Of course, that isn't the case. The best designers
concern themselves with the why not just the how.

When I published the first volume of Book of Ideas, I enjoyed
a constant flurry of emails and questions about many pieces
of work, including the book cover.

This time, I wanted to get one step ahead. You can find the
new volume's cover design case study at the back of this book
to give you both answers to the "why" and "how" it was made.

Client
Hartridges

Type
Carry pack design

SINCE 1882 · SINCE 1882 · SINCE 1882 · SINCE 1882

DELICIOUSLY DRY, BOTANICAL TASTE MADE WITH NATURAL FLAVOURS

HARTRIDGES

BRITISH SOFT DRINKS Co.

Indian
TONIC WATER

Gluten free & suitable for vegans.

4x 200ml

"My great great grandfather started making our delicious soft drinks in the rolling hills of Hampshire in 1882 and I'm proud to follow his footsteps. I hope you enjoy these drinks."

Edward Hartridge

Client
Hartridges

Type
Label design update

Various logos
Design

THE
GREEN
DEN

PLAY . STORAGE . GROW

234

DIMENSION

LÖWE

exerceo

ViceSecurity
Part of the Vice Security Group

inhere

Various logos
Design

journei
life beyond boundaries

CARMINE
ROSE

klein

10

BOND IN MOTION
THE LARGEST OFFICIAL COLLECTION OF ORIGINAL JAMES BOND VEHICLES
007

AS | **ALICE STRANGE**

rest **&** be

NOVEMBER
UNIVERSE
by BRAND NU
ORIGINAL
SUPPLY
STORE

True & Original
Stein Garten
Bavarian Beerhouse & Restaurant
Est. 2014

SPEAKING THE LANGUAGE

Verbal communication is a gift, one all the sweeter when you consider how colourful, layered and beautifully inventive it can be. Language evolves constantly, swelling with new terms and expressions.

Every creative connection or solution starts with a discussion. You need to get to know your subject matter before you can begin to consider how to visually solve the problem. A great design is a two-thirds conversation and one-third creativity.

I've learned to love presenting strategies, mood boards and design proposals. This is my chance to explain myself along with the direction I offer to take. People listen, ask questions and the dialogue builds in the right way. Everyone feels involved in the early stages is an integral part of the process and in making it a success.

If I work with clients who aren't local or there's no time to set up a meeting, I simply record a video walkthrough to show every little detail and explain myself. Unlike in the boardroom, people don't feel pressured to make snap judgments, throwaway suggestions or develop a sudden hatred towards elements of work they've never seen before. They have time to replay the video, digest it and come back with consolidated feedback. This process is genuinely golden: it works every time.

When I'm working with remote freelancers or developers, I don't waste anyone's time writing long emails to describe every single tweak or change. We jump into a screen-sharing online meeting to talk through every detail there and then. Everyone saves time, and the project improves through discussion – we can point at each other's screen and directly discuss the areas that need attention. Nothing gets lost in translation.

When you're faced with what seems like a near-impossible task to solve, take the time to think about how you can best tell a story on behalf of your client. Once you can articulate and visualise their imaginations, you get to lead the process and will soon stop making work that might instantly be shred to pieces.

Client
Seraclimb

Type
Branding

WHAT DOES CREATIVITY MEAN TO YOU?

On the eve of my first CreativeMornings talk, the team in Edinburgh asked me for an ice-breaker question to be printed on attendees' badges. The topic was Transparency, and I struggled for a while to come up with something that felt right. As my talk was going to be an honest account of what I do, and because I'm naturally quite a nosey person, I opted for 'what does creativity mean to you?'

The answers were fascinating, with responses ranging from freedom to money, influence, satisfaction, expression and happiness. One person simply said "everything". It's such a simple question, with as many possible answers as they are people on this planet. There's no right or wrong, but people who have their creative philosophy clear seem to find better efficiency, satisfaction and purpose in their work.

When I look back at my career over the years, I realise I was, at times, lacking a true purpose. My creative work was initially about supporting my existence – a job to pay the rent. It worked. But when I progressed a little, I worked for my soul to ensure I get an emotional return on the time I spent on a project. Realising I could use my skills and knowledge to help others unlock their potential was a revelation.

Every day I aim to smash the myth that creativity is lost in adulthood. We don't lose that magic spark, it's just not often at the forefront of our increasingly busy lives. But creativity comes in many guises: when I see the hard-hitting yet humorous protest signs that people make to express their feelings and opinions, I only wish I was as half as creative as the ones who made those placards. What we create might not be destined to start a global movement or change, but if just one person finds it useful, well-designed or inspirational then it's a job well done. When a client becomes an inspired and empowered friend, it's even better.

So what does creativity mean to me? I believe we can change the world one day at a time by doing the best work possible. Just as a protest sign can make others feel stronger, we should aim to make our mark on the world and inspire others to pick up their tools and make a difference.

Client
Raleigh Ritchie

Type
Single Artwork

RALEIGH RITCHIE   LONELY SUMMER

CREATIVITY FOR FREE?

I wanted to be a rock star when I was 13. I saved from a few dull part-time jobs, bought my first bass guitar and formed a band with a few friends. When we were offered opportunities to play as a support band for the big boys, we didn't hesitate for a second. From one simple decision, we quickly went on to play to a crowd of a few hundred metalheads when I was only a few days short of my 15th birthday. I guess I don't need to mention that we didn't even think of getting paid, we were there to have a good time – we were poor, but we were the ones on stage. The buzz of playing live made us want to be better.

Since those teenage shows, I've done countless things in life and work where I've just been happy to have the opportunity to experience something new. I worked many shitty jobs to ensure I could afford to chase my interests, passion and future career.

The magic of doing something for free is that you can really let go. Once the money is involved, the sandpit is set aside and the real work begins. Money changes people and their expectations on both sides of the transaction.

Working for free in the creative industries will always be a hot topic. We have to judge the opportunity given to us; and there will always be vultures trying to persuade you to give up your time for their benefit, not yours.

However, take a moment to consider how much internet content would exist if people had been paid to create it all: how many video tutorials, Medium articles, Github open source code, blog posts and Pinterest boards would be available if people expected remuneration for it all? We create passion content and services for us and for others to enjoy.

Generosity can pay dividends.

Client
Raleigh Ritchie

Type
Single Artwork

CHRIS LOCO & RALEIGH RITCHIE

THE RIVER

MIND THE GAP

Client
Raleigh Ritchie

Type
Album artwork

In collaboration with
Tamas Arpadi

When I was given the first demos for the Mind the Gap EP, I felt spoilt for choice with potential visual meanings. Raleigh Ritchie's lyrics are full of raw storytelling – tales of failed relationships, depression, obsessiveness or failing to integrate into society – so his lyrics gave me tons of ideas right from the off. To help me formulate the art direction strategy for this release, I started compiling visual references to support my treatment script. I'm a big fan of Erwin Wurm, the prolific Austrian artist is known for inspiring expressive art which is rich in juxtapositions and surreal double meanings.

I spoke to Jacob [Anderson, Ritchie's real name] on the phone, while he was filming one of the series of Game of Thrones in Northern Ireland. Jacob – who plays Grey Worm in the series – doesn't like to be featured on his covers, and this project was perfect for keeping it that way.

I wanted to build a simulation of a TV chat show in 3D. But this set also featured padded cells, sword fighting wedding cakes on legs, a therapist's room and a bedroom that would morph into an open street, as well as a few other scenarios. It all oozed with elaborate detail but seemed to fail to deliver the desired impact. We started stripping away layers until we ended up with individual items that looked like gallery pieces for each song's artwork. It was time to use very little to say a lot.

Once we got to this point of simplicity, the production picked up the pace. Most of the images were quickly taking shape – the hamster wheel was even done in one take. However, the cover artwork took the best part of 20 options to get it right. Nothing was sticking.

Each Cinema 4D model rendered in the gold material was retouched in Adobe Photoshop to achieve the super gloss inverted colours, applied with the Selective Colour adjustment layer to remove the black tones from the black channels, replacing them with cyan and yellow to give the shadows a greenish contrasting holographic tone.

Some of the unused test ideas are included in this case study too. This was one of the first few projects where I got the explore the full possibilities of 3D modelling and it signalled a new beginning.

Client
Raleigh Ritchie

Project
Mind the Gap EP

Client
Raleigh Ritchie

Image
'Sicko'

Client
Raleigh Ritchie

Image
'Motions'

Client
Raleigh Ritchie

Image
'Strait Jacket'

Client
Raleigh Ritchie

Image
'Unicron Loev'

Client
Raleigh Ritchie

Image
'Liability'

Client
Raleigh Ritchie

Image
'unused'

Client
Raleigh Ritchie

Image
'unused'

TWO HOURS TO CHANGE FUTURE

Client
Porganic

Type
Packaging

There's no telling how successful a project will be when it goes out the door. You just have to hope that the hours and love you poured in will create something more than a lukewarm reaction. Most often though, that's what you get: people like it, but they don't go nuts for it. Then occasionally, there are times when you literally spend a couple of hours on quick doodles, sketches or tests and the world goes mad for the work. This project was one of those.

Just before Christmas, I was commissioned to develop a new brand of lemonade in three different flavours for the US market. I've learned better than to say that I don't work over holidays any more – and this was my daughter's first Christmas. However, I wanted to make it work, so I offered to submit a single route pitch after the holiday. My art direction was based on the idea of the exclusivity of the brand's ingredients. Based on my research of the products out there, I didn't feel we needed to explicitly depict each ingredient. Instead, I chose to use colour cues to let consumers make their own minds up, and associate the packaging with what's in the bottle. I never take customers, clients or consumers for fools or geniuses: it's about creating interest and engendering some emotion around the product.

My route work didn't win for one simple reason: it fell 0.4% behind the other design proposal in the focus group research. It scored very positively on all fronts, but the client decided to run with the packaging design that had the higher score.

I wanted to share the work in my folio as there's something about it, even though it was made in just a few hours. When I published the work online and on social, people loved it.

The project has been generating new business enquiries on a weekly basis ever since. It's been featured across industry magazines, design sites and countless Instagram-curated blogs. Given the positive feedback and reactions from thousands of people, I've started making enquiries into how to turn these designs into a reality and start my own lemonade company. It's not my priority right now, but it's amazing how a couple of hours on a design pitch can change the direction of future decisions.

Client
Porganic

Image
**Tangerine
Lemonade**

porganic™

P

original

LEMONADE

proud to be hand crafted in
small batches by artisan
bottlers in California

12FL OZ / 355ml

porganic™

P

blackberry

LEMONADE

proud to be hand crafted in
small batches by artisan
bottlers in California

12FL OZ / 355ml

Client
Porganic

Image
**Blackberry
Lemonade**

porganic™

Client
Porganic

Image
**Blackberry
Lemonade**

Client
Porganic

Image
**Original
Lemonade**

porganic™

P

original

LEMONADE

proud to be hand crafted in
small batches by artisan
bottlers in California

12 FL OZ / 355 ml

Client
Porganic

Image
**Original
Lemonade**

porganic™

P

COKE + ADOBE + YOU

Project
Personal

Type
Illustration

In collaboration with
Tamas Arpadi

Even though schedules can be relentless when you're working on numerous projects at once, it's imperative to find at least half an hour before the end of the day to just test out some of your ideas. Doing something quick and rewarding is vital to keep you happy, and without it, many self-initiated projects would simply never happen. Month-long projects don't offer up an instant boost like quick, playful experimentation can. These sessions can also help you mentally check out from the rest of the working day. **Stand Proud and Represent** was produced for the Coke x Adobe x Tokyo Olympics call for entries. It can be tempting to jump right in with a brief like this one. When you couple something as iconic as the Coke bottle shape with a Japanese theme, certain very obvious ideas will come to the fore. A lot of fantastic work had also recently been created for the Coke bottle's 125th anniversary and quickly researching those struck off ideas that had already been done.

The key was to keep rethinking and validating the concept. There were lots of ideas to work through, including one that would see the Coke bottles animated with cherry blossom, but the initial outcome felt more like kaleidoscopic, psychedelic 60s art rather than something meaningful for the Tokyo Olympics.

After a few weeks of a quick 3D render tests, the final route began to emerge. The first decision was to run with a theme of national teams who fight to the last minute, to make their country proud. Based on the number of players in a football team, we had eleven bottles arranged in a lineup. I saw them as standing still on the pitch, listening to their national anthem, ready to go out and give it their all.

The second route was a homage to a Japanese deity called Kannon. Her symbol, a peacock, represents compassion and kind-heartedness. It only felt fitting to align this to the spirit of sporting fair play. For the images, the Coke bottle was duplicated and repositioned to create the effect of peacock wings in a heart shape.

Since there was no deadline as such for this project, it was great to take the time to produce something worthwhile, with meaning, rather than sharing hasty work. There are no prizes for being the quickest in such projects.

Project
Coke x Adobe x You

Image
**Stand Proud and
Represent**

Project
Coke x Adobe x You

Image
**Stand Proud and
Represent**

Project
Coke x Adobe x You

Image
Kannon

AM:PM
PM:AM

Client
FormFiftyFive

Type
Album artwork

In collaboration with
Tamas Arpadi

Online magazine Made by Folk (previously called Form Fifty Five)
invites designers around the world to compile a 55-track playlist on
Spotify, garnering all sorts of weird and wonderful collections
of creatives' favourite tunes, old and new.

For my playlist, I wanted to compile songs that summarise the mood
of a working day or night. Our days can start gently, then rapidly head
into a crazy midday rush. My playlist, titled AM:PM, looked to reflect
the arc of moods and feelings in a single day.

I never like to do things by halves – there's always something extra
you can add to make a project more memorable. This one was no
different: a simple idea for a playlist cover turned into two weeks
of experiments to bring an idea based on abstract typography to life.
One playlist turned into two, totalling 110 songs.

I wanted to experiment with isometric angles and different
perspectives to build up objects that only loosely join together
for the intended letterform. There was meant to be a tradeoff
between legibility and abstraction.

All changes for this project were done via screen -share, without
the need for constant feedback emails. The final colour choices
were inspired by high-end tailoring materials found on the inside
of a really classy suit jacket.

The initial test work turned out rather well, but it was too easy to
see the final image – perhaps a strange problem to encounter.
The image was intended to embody the concept of the "right wrong"
– something that doesn't feel right at first, but the more you study
and explore it, takes on a greater meaning.

It took a lot of different versions to get the right balance,
but the "right wrong" idea won out.

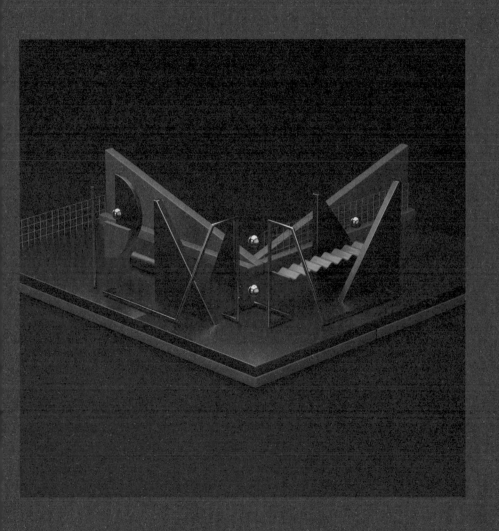

Project
AM:PM PM:AM

Image
PM:AM

Project
AM:PM PM:AM

Image
AM:PM

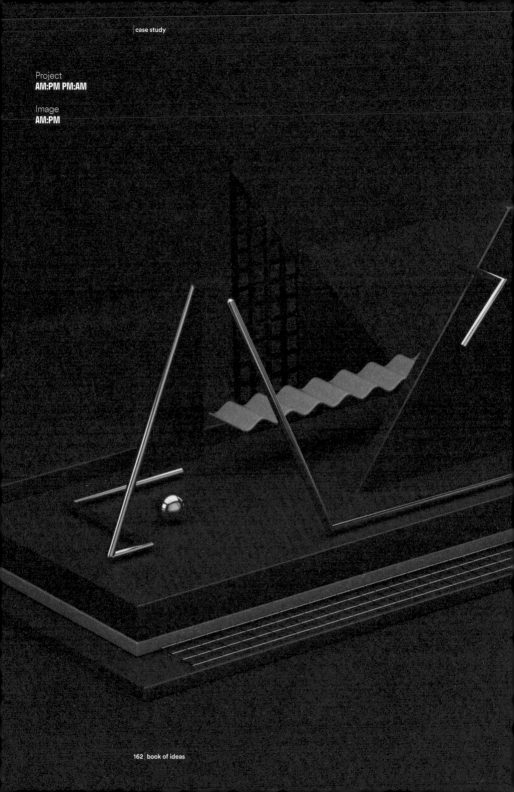

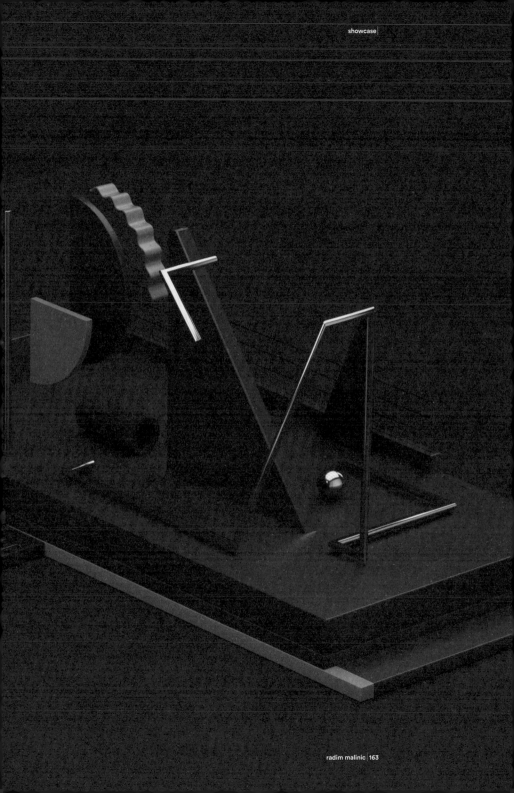

WHAT COLOUR CAN YOU HEAR?

Client
Krysta Youngs

Type
Album artwork

In collaboration with
Craig Minchington

Album cover artwork has shrunk from predominantly gracing 12-inch vinyl to being forced into tiny digital thumbnails. However, its job remains the same; and it's painful to see so many bad cover designs out there that far from justifying the music.

Thanks to the likes of Spotify, we've got so much new music at our fingertips it can feel overwhelming: that's where the cover design has to work hardest, enticing you to check out an artist you'd never heard of before.

Krysta Youngs has been an ongoing collaborator for the best part of ten years. She's a strong, bold songwriter and deserves the same from her cover art. Independent souls like Krysta naturally have a lot of opinions on how the work should look.

When we had our first Skype call to discuss initial ideas, we talked about objects that could represent the themes and lyrics – some were derived from music video treatments, and some from the stories that inspired the conception of her tracks.

We also touched on the topic of colour choices. I suggested we give the first single to people with synesthesia to help us decipher the colour choice. It turns out that people in LA have the biggest occurrences of synesthesia in the world, apparently, but eventually we found a producer who gave us a credible answer to the colours he "saw" when hearing the album's title track: deep red, maroon and cherry tones.

That information was invaluable: we no longer had to doubt our colour choices for that release, or any of the others.

Client
Krysta Youngs

Type
**Singles
artwork**

Client
Krysta Youngs

Type
Logo design

YOUNGS

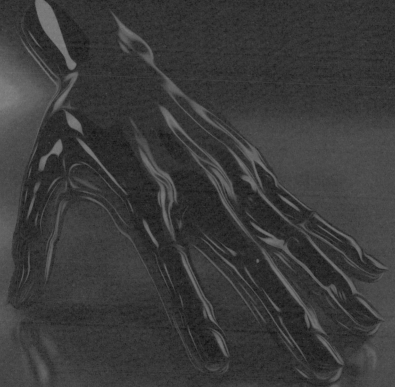

UNDER MY SKIN

MIND

Our minds can often feel like they are running on overdrive, working double shifts and refusing to hit the pause button.

The **Mind** section looks into finding the benefits of working in silence, breaking stale everyday habits, identifying your weaknesses, staying in the present moment and keeping your mind in check.

MAKE YOUR RULES, FOLLOW THEM

As a creative person, you might not feel that you want to follow the rules: no-one likes being told what to do, let alone what not to do. I love reading interviews with people who feel liberated enough to break all the rules and bend reality to their favour – I used to be of the same conviction.

I wanted to go my own way and be as rebellious as possible.

Anarchy can be beautiful, but it isn't always useful: if you start a riot, you have to know where to go with it. It's only by making your own rules that you can honestly be true to yourself, and make a lasting impression with what you stand for. Only you can decide how you wish to apply the method to your madness.

Choose what makes you excited: find the best way to work, where you feel most at home, which ways of working will help you benefit from your efforts and lead to success.

If your rules don't work, you can change them.

But when you keep following your own rules, endless new directions will open up: you'll put a stop to your endless battles to break other people's rules when you set them for yourself.

Make your rules, follow them.

CREATIVE ATHLETE

When the cameras zoom in on an athlete at the starting block, we see someone about to run the race that might change their life. Behind the scenes, a team of sports psychologists, trainers, physios and others have worked tirelessly towards this moment: that athlete is there to prove their innumerable personal sacrifices and preparation worked. Ready, set, go...

Everyone in the creative industries should be just like that athlete. We're here to give it our all: every single day we should cherish being able to create something that matters to us, that we can take pride in. But unlike that athlete, we haven't always got a team behind the scenes preparing us for gold. We have to invest our own time in the growth and development that'll give us the chance to improve our work every day. Being a better creative is not only about making sure you know what the latest software feature or plug-in can add to your workflow. It's about understanding all aspects of creative disciplines and how they connect together. You can only become a better creative when you go out and learn.

As a creative athlete, you will learn how to understand the process of delivering your work and get the right reaction. Understand what makes others tick: learn how to tell better stories and make people fall in love with your work by explaining what went into the process. Show the offcuts that didn't make the proposal. Share the behind-the-scenes.

A creative athlete stays focused. Learn to be more efficient and plan your time better. Write lists. To-do apps are a waste of time, use pen and paper. Stop browsing shit websites when you're at work. Surround yourself with people – some who are inspiring, others who could be little bit lost. Learn from the ambitious ones, and think about how you can inspire the wayward souls. Seeing both sides will stop you from becoming disillusioned.

Treat every project like the Olympics. Not every project will justify all the extra work and effort, but it should matter to you. These aren't "lost hours", it's an investment in building your creative muscle. You never know when you might hit your personal best, or when you might win gold.

Project
Miracle Gin

Type
Packaging design

KNOW YOUR ENEMY WITHIN

We all have our idols, yet when we see their illustrious careers we don't see the struggles and battles behind their achievements.

It can feel like the world wants you to "follow your passion", "dream big", be a "girl boss", a "top biller". But there aren't too many motivational quotes out there encouraging you to look at yourself and honestly evaluate what's working against you, to really ask if you're ok right now.

We all have emotional baggage. I hated feeling like I was the only person struggling with inner demons; it felt like everyone else was doing perfectly fine. Mental health issues can make your world feel so very small and lonely; but the more you look around, the more you realise we're all bundles of anxious energy.

The most liberating way to deal with the enemy within you is to be open about it. It's ok to say you're not ok, it's important to seek help.

I needed counselling at one point in my life. In my last session, I was told that the ducks will never line up in life. At first, I sat in disbelief, then I got it: fear and anxiety might never go away. But once we've identified them, we're better equipped to deal with them every time they rear their ugly heads.

It's not fun to stand up to your enemies on your own, and sharing your own journey with others might help give you the tools to fight them.

It's imperative to know your dreams, even more so to understand what might stop you from achieving them.

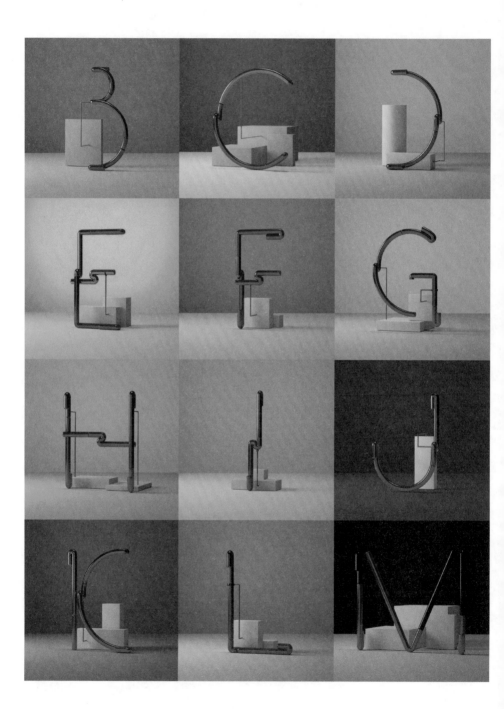

WANT TO BE FAMOUS? THINK AGAIN

The design industry is paved with no shortage of awards and accolades. It's certainly satisfying to know that someone somewhere thought your work was good enough to win one.

But is this a path to fame? Not so much.

Life in the industry limelight can open many doors: your work is seen by more people, and conference invites, interview requests, award judging duties and other opportunities come knocking. That's the good part.

But there are two sides to every story. Every piece of new work is now judged by everyone out there. Every self-appointed critic has an opinion, simply because they now feel entitled to have one. I've heard pub discussions about creatives no one there ever met, but they acted like these designers owed them something. It seems like as a known artist or designer, you're meant to be creating work for everyone, that must be to all their tastes. Twitter becomes shark-infested waters, teeming with judgment. The more public your work, the more it forms the focus of a spectator sport open to those who may or may not understand the processes behind it.

We elevate our contemporaries to "industry famous"' status, though only significant to a tiny echo chamber. I doubt my mother will have heard of any "famous" designers working today. That doesn't stop lots of people peacocking around trying very, very hard to use their creativity to become famous without really knowing what they have to say.

The limelight is a vehicle for having your work recognised, but it won't make you enjoy the process any more. Enjoy your craft: be a reluctant celebrity.

Project
36 days of type

Type
Custom type

POWER OF QUIET

When was the last time you found a quiet spot to move
away from life's noise to think, sit and simply be in the
present moment?

For a long time, I didn't know how to exist in silence. A life-long
love of music provided a non-stop soundtrack to almost every
minute of my life. As a teenager I used to go to sleep with
headphones on listening to death metal – music much faster
than my resting heart rate rushing through my head – yet it
felt therapeutic.

Music can be an excellent creative trigger, and give you the
energy boost to push a deadline across the finish line. But while
music was and still is an exhilarating part of my life every day,
sometimes when you need to really think, that extra noise
and information can act as interference.

When you no longer get briefs to follow but are only provided
with small fractions of information to work with, time is needed
to understand the questions, to have space to simply think of
about how to make your next move.

Sometimes clients can be vague and that can be very beneficial:
the blanks have to be filled in and the creative brief built, art
direction set and the design strategy outlined. For that, I need
silence to help me find answers, to give me space to think and
work it all out. I need to be alone with my thoughts to find the
most direct way to a solution.

A creative mind is easily distracted. For that reason, I can't work
out of a coffee shop or any other public space: I can't focus on
much more than the space and buzz around me. Our lives are full
of loud noise and often we simply turn up the volume on what we
want to hear. Consider occasionally nudging the volume down,
making the noise disappear, even for just a short while. Enjoy
the power of a quiet moment.

I PREFER THE

TUMULT OF LIBERTY

TO THE

QUIET OF SERVITUDE

ORIGINAL ARTWORK SERIES. DESIGNED BY RADIM MALINIC/ BRAND NU IN LONDON, ENGLAND

Radim Malinic

REPEAT, REPEAT, REPEAT

When a streaming service's autoplay function kicks in,
more often than not, we impatient binge-watchers let it play on.
Sometimes we even help it by clicking the play button –
15 seconds can feel like a long time. The option to keep getting
closer to the season finale is way too enticing, and it's so easy.

Next!

Digital content is truly overwhelming: we consume it without
paying too much attention to what we just watched or listened
to. We no longer focus on one thing at a time, and in doing so, we
miss so much detail. We half-read blog articles and career towards
RSI with relentless swipes of our phone screens. While clever
software engineers play a not-insignificant role in all this, ultimately
we're the ones making the decision to keep on clicking, despite
every platform doing its utmost to stop us leaving.

Attention span? Next!

How often do we really take time to fully appreciate something?
How often do you click the repeat button?

When you read, watch or listen to something, you should
spend time thinking about, discussing and deciphering it,
and recommend it to others if it's worth it.

There's magic in discovering something you missed the first time
around. Take an episode of your favourite podcast or TV series,
listen to an album or rewatch a movie.

Give yourself a day or two's break between each session and
repeat. You'll be rewarded no end discovering the information you
missed; you'll find something new every time. We need to relearn
how to focus: only then can we truly enjoy the present moment
and what it has to offer.

Project
68 - Personal

Type
Custom type

Client
Ecstasy of Gold

Type
**Branding
+ Design**

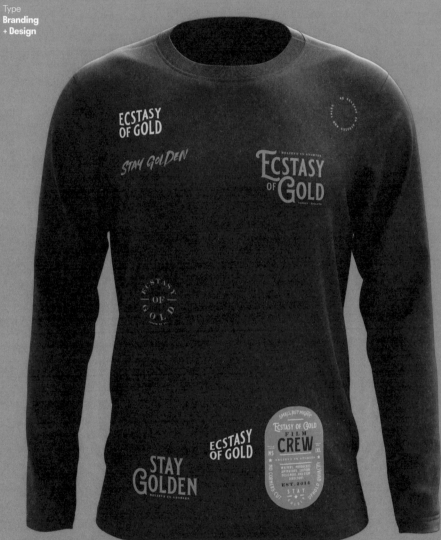

THE ART OF LETTING GO

We should be the masters of our destiny, yet sometimes it feels like we aren't the ones calling the shots. We're being led by others – directors, managers, clients or customers – and when this happens it's time to rise above the situation and practise the art of letting go of things. Not every customer is going to be compatible every time. Some people can start off great, and soon turn into startlingly tricky individuals. Some clients think that working with a creative practitioner provides them with an unlimited number of changes, versions and iterations for the exchange of a small sum. But there should always be a way out of a stressful scenario.

Always try to make sure the work you produce follows steps that remove potential headaches and unnecessary back-and-forths in favour of enjoyable, constructive collaboration. Before any work starts, put a contract in place to spell out the number of rounds and revisions you're willing to do. You can get a template from the internet or ask a lawyer to help you.

I remember the first time I decided to let a client go, weighing up my sanity against my bank balance. The project fee was meant to be quite huge, but not as huge as the trouble brewing ahead. It was becoming obvious that I would potentially come out with a loss – the project was going to overrun quite spectacularly. I had a lot less experience back then, but I'm glad I made that call. It felt liberating but very scary at the same time: rent was due in a couple of weeks. The gamble paid off, and I was lucky to start a different project only two days later. Thankfully, I was available to take the project.

I believe in karma. Every time I've have had to make a difficult decision to turn down work or terminate a genuinely unpleasant project, it seems to have led to better things.

We create work that we want people to use, enjoy and cherish so that clients come back and keep hiring us again and again. There's a time and place to go above and beyond to deliver the best possible work we can. But be careful – always respect yourself and your career. When the time comes, say no and let go. Don't let the bastards grind you down.

Project
November Universe

Image
THNX bag

EVERYDAY DIFFERENT

A certain type of TV advert crops up regularly, with a rapid succession of shots to illustrate how much we need a particular product to kick-start our morning: eyes open, the alarm is stopped, shower, dress, leave the house, get into the car/onto the train, arrive at work, call the lift, start the computer, put the kettle on. It succinctly sums up the morning routine of the population.

This sequence highlights our dependency on caffeine, shower gel, how much we love the smell of a new car and so on to get us going. It also underscores the sameness we expect from each day. But if you're lucky, today might be a little bit different to yesterday – and not just in what new biscuits are lurking in the studio. We're lucky that creative work can provide variation, but that's not a guarantee.

You might be doing the same thing over and over again, and autopilot takes over. When we do the same thing repeatedly, the time it takes to complete that task can feel shorter thanks to its familiarity. When we perform a repetitive task our brain fills in the blanks to save energy: it recognises the moments when things look and feel similar, and it gives our minds a break from processing them. But shaking things up, even slightly, every day can keep us focused.

I was once told, "make sure you go take a different route to work every morning". While I'm all for efficiency, it makes perfect sense. When I started walking my usual routes anticlockwise I soon found myself getting lost – courses I could once map with my eyes closed became strangely unfamiliar. Soon I began to see details that had gone unnoticed for most of the time I walked London's streets.

This experience made me rethink the way I live and work. Challenging ourselves not to make the same choices all the time can be an extremely inspiring long term. Switch off your autopilot and figure out what you can do differently.

Project
Experiment

Type
Design

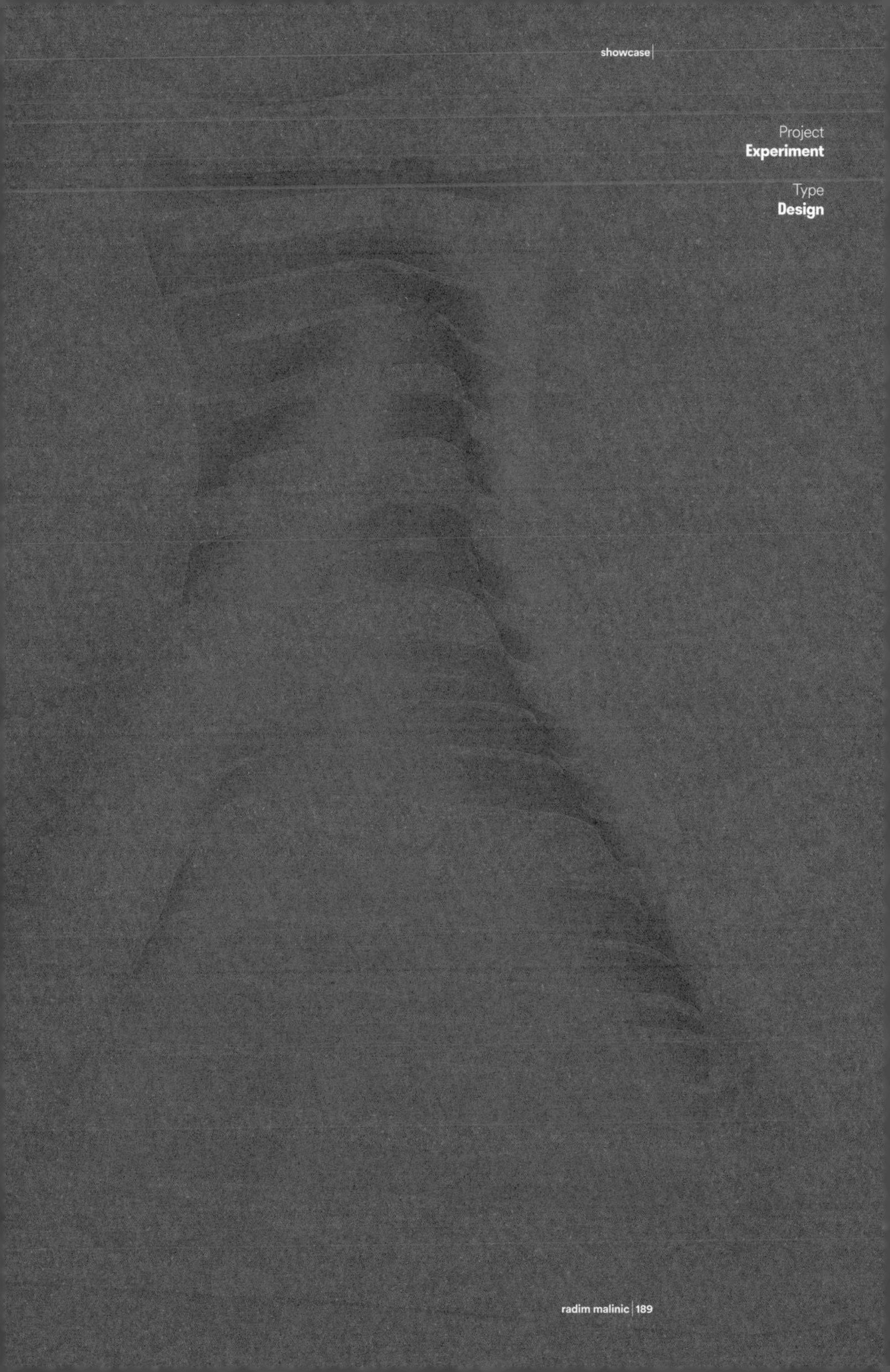

ON STAYING HUMBLE

How many times a day do you pinch yourself at the realisation that creativity is your job? Sure, it's not always plain sailing, but it pays to be grateful that we have the opportunity to do something that can bring so much enjoyment as a career.

I treat every project, and the people involved in it, with respect.

And while it's important to be confident, knowledgeable and professional – demonstrating a real passion to really immerse yourself in the work – it's easy to get it wrong. Don't be too big for your boots, or tip confidence into arrogance – cockiness won't get you far.

Reputation is hard to gain and even harder to fix. When you keep your feet on the ground, you'll save yourself a lot of back-paddling in the future.

To some people, a little bit of success can bring a much-needed confidence boost, to others it could be an overdose for their ego.

We are not bigger or better than one another, we are equal and different. Stay cool. Stay humble.

Project
November Universe

Type
Product design

SOHO

NOVEMBER
UNIVERSE
by BRAND NU
ORIGINAL
SUPPLY
STORE

LESSONS IN COMPASSION

How often do you take time to understand how those around you are feeling? Are you invested in other people's worlds as much as your own?

Knowing how to read other people is an invaluable creative asset. Taking time to see the world from the viewpoint of your partner, friends, colleagues or clients can forge new connections and stop us making rash decisions as we take a more compassionate approach to our life and work.

I've been in the creative industry for long enough to have met some incredible people that genuinely care about others and want them to succeed. I'm still picking myself up from meeting David Carson – the nicest man I've ever met. There are good souls out there, and this is my homage to them.

I've also been in the creative industry long enough to have come across some people who are quite the opposite: people bursting with ego, who instead of cheering on others simply spread spite. I always wonder what the world be like if all that negative bullshit energy was channelled into something productive.

By seeing the world through the eyes of others we can start to comprehend what might have been obscured by our own version of reality. No two people see the world identically. Whoever you meet, make them feel welcome and understood. It might change the course of their day.

We believe we lead hectic lives, packed to the rafters with no room for others apart from our closest friends and family.

This is why we have to make the space for others, to understand what's going on outside our little own space.

After all, you reap what you sow.

Project
November Universe

Type
Typography

ECHO

NOVEMBER
UNIVERSE
by BRAND NU
ORIGINAL
SUPPLY
STORE

BE HERE NOW

The English are renowned for their ability to form an orderly
queue – it can look and feel like silent poetry. Sometimes. I was
once in a tense, angry Post Office queue, with a little old lady at
the front. After a long wait, she dithered for a few short seconds
when a loud voice from the back yelled, 'pay attention!' The
poetry illusion was shattered, and the English language's capacity
to be at once rude and polite was made plain. Those two words
have stayed with me ever since. It made me think more broadly
about how even the most razor-sharp focus can so easily slip.

It's widely recognised that creativity can have a therapeutic
effect on our wellbeing. But for a while, it felt like the opposite:
I was fussing so much about everything else around my work
that I didn't pay attention to what I was creating.

My head was everywhere but in the here and now.

Although I learned to meditate as a teenager in my psychology
class, I didn't put it into practice until my early 30s. I couldn't
concentrate, my mind was racing, and I needed to reconnect
with my inner self before I hit full-on burnout. Meditation was
a way to find my focus again, how to stay in the present moment,
which turned from a sticking plaster solution into an essential
part of showing me how to enjoy life again.

Try to experience each moment when it is happening. Focus on
reading each word, take in the smell of this book, consider how
it feels to the touch. Ignore your phone and inbox for a while.

Do the same in your next piece of work.
Enjoy every single part of it.

Be here now.

TIME FOR
TEA

A BISCUIT

BRAND NU / ORIGINAL ARTWORK SERIES /

DESIGNED BY RADIM MALINIC

SLEEP WHEN YOU SLEEP, WORK WHEN YOU WORK

When you start to learn a new language, at some point the day will come when you have your first foreign language dream. It's magical, and you can feel yourself making real headway. A similar thing can happen when you get into the world of creativity, and solutions can sometimes prove to be nocturnal.

That's fun until sleep stops being sleep: when you would wake up after eight hours and feel worse than if you'd slept for half that time. It can be increasingly harder to get a good rest, and as you can become more and more tired it can be harder to make good work, too. You can feel trapped in an infinite cycle.

That's why we need to learn how to leave work in the studio and life outside of it. Once you stop daydreaming and focus on keeping those things separate, better work and peace of mind gradually arrive in tandem.

Plan your day's work, rest and life so they have a pre-set time in your day. When you finish work, write a list of projects for the next day. Check out and move on, otherwise, life and work will be in constant battle with one another.

When workloads are heavy and deadlines are looming, we start to fantasise about having time off right in the middle of the working day. Then when we get to rest, our minds are spinning with work thoughts again. This is why we think there's no work/life balance.

We think we're the wisest creatures on the planet. But take big cats, for example – when they sleep they don't think about hunting. Neither are they thinking about sleeping when they're chasing their prey. Let's learn from them.

When you work, work.
When you rest, rest.
When you sleep, sleep.

Project
Personal

Type
**Poster
design**

Project
36 days of type for November Universe

Type
T-shirt design

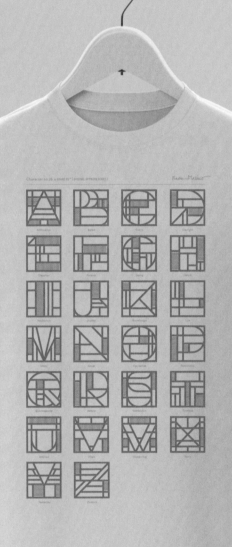

YOU ARE WHO YOU SHOULD BE

When I get up in the morning, there's nothing that makes me happier than putting on odd socks. And of course there's a little method to my madness: I prefer green, yellow or blue on my left foot and red, orange and purple on the other. I've been wearing them this way for the best part of my life.

For the last few years, I've even stepped things up by wearing odd coloured trainers. When I notice people looking down at my feet when we pass each other on the street, I know that even in that tiny fraction of their day, they've spent time thinking about what they've seen. It's my "thing", just as I have a signature style in my work. I am me.

It's hard to enter the creative industries without feeling anxious about the legacy that preceded us. So much great work has already been created, and more are being produced every day. It can feel like everyone, literally, everyone is bringing their 'A' game. It can be so easy to buy into the belief that everyone is a genius.

The truth is the opposite. Great people are just at a different place in their own journeys. We make our own unique work because we each have our own personality and beliefs.

We should embrace individuality, but being different can feel scary at first. It makes you stick out, and that brings attention, but it doesn't make you wrong. Don't worry what others might think, or if they're wary of odd socks.

The key is tapping into our inner voice and producing work right from the heart. Write down what makes you unique, pin it to the wall and be proud of it. You are who you should be: enjoy every minute of it.

Client
Ark+UBS

Type
Invitation design

Sir Paul Marshall, Chair of Ark Schools, **invites you to**

DARING TO BE

Tuesday 31 January 2017
RSA House, 8 John Adam St, London WC2N 6EZ

7pm	Drinks
7.45pm	Dinner
10pm	Carriages

Nearly half of all children across the world leave primary school without being able to read, write, or do basic maths. That is 250 million young people who have been denied a fair start in life.

Join UBS and Ark for an opportunity to hear how Ark's Education Partnerships Group supports governments and other partners to address some of the systemic challenges that hinder the delivery of quality education across Africa and beyond.

This intimate dinner will give you an insight into our vision for a better education for all children, our current and future projects, and how you can support us.

 RSVP by Wednesday 4 January

INVENT YOUR DREAM FUTURE

When I got a job as a junior designer, I only needed to be good enough for the job position on that day. No one really cared how much better I could be – as long as the work was getting signed off by clients, everything was fine. Pretty quickly, I realised that I need to push myself to improve my skills, thinking and process. I needed to do it for myself, to keep being interested in my work and maintain the creativity in what was supposed to be a creative role.

I spent a lot of time working on my own stuff around full-time employment. The long nights were worth it: without practice, there's no progress. After weeks, months and years of honing my skills, learning and experimenting I felt I was ready to take on a bigger role and even bigger projects. But when I started applying for other jobs, I wasn't getting any of them. It was pretty devastating, but luckily it turned out to be a blessing in disguise.

I went out alone, and through my own freelance work, I started building a steady clientele. All of a sudden, I was once again charmed by the prospect of creating work that excited me, my clients and their customers. I could choose what clients, projects and opportunities I wanted to take on to shape my future and creative business. Through being refused a job at an agency, I opened the agency of my dreams.

I will always be grateful for the time when I was an in-house designer: I needed it and I learned a lot. It also showed me that I was the sole person who could make my career happen. It's only when you have to deal with all the knocks that come with running your own show that you learn how to pick yourself up and make things happen.

Life should not be about trying to fit a job description. We are here to create work that we will be remembered for. If you don't fit the mould, create a vision of your own ideal career. The best stuff in life doesn't come to us by chance, we have to make it happen. Everyone can make the work of their dreams and invent their dream career, one that will keep you excited for years to come.

Client
DunnHumby

Type
Logo design

In collaboration with
Craig Minchington

SEASONS CHANGE

The moment it feels like we identify our calling in life can be truly, monumentally magical. You've searched high and low, you got lost a few times and now you're here. The next challenge, surely, is to hold onto it.

But our callings and careers can be multifaceted and continuously evolving. There's no such thing as forever in the creative world. Depending on your curiosity, interest and grit, you might be happy to stick with the same type of work for a lifetime, or make it seem like a fleeting moment.

Life brings house moves, weddings, children, pets, interests, hobbies, travel and much more: all those will have some effect on who you are and what you do. They might bring a new outlook on life, give you a new idea or two and keep things interesting. Unhappy times and life dramas are inevitable too, and we have to adapt to everything that comes our way and how it might change us.

Maybe at some point you were convinced you'd be an illustrator for life, but the next moment you're art director, then you're in charge of your own studio and all the hiring and firing that entails. Maybe you leave for a tech startup, UX design or even developer position: all involve different skills but the same core passion. Every transformation can be exciting but also remarkably testing: when you've worked so hard on making one thing happen, why change?

Regardless of your situation, use your time wisely and maximise your output. Get lost in your craft and explore every minute of your available time. We can't go back in time: we have to enjoy all that life and a creative career have to offer, and strive to do our best in both.

Seasons change, and there's no such thing as a 'bad' one.
Each brings unique excitement, challenges and rewards.
The only inevitability is change.

Client
Inner City Sound Clash

Type
**Album artwork
+ Typography**

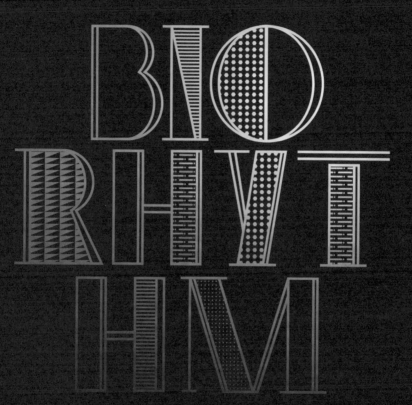

1. **INTRO / BIORHYTHM**   2. **WHAT GOES AROUND** feat REUBEN   3. **PRESS PLAY** feat JAIDENE VEDA AND RISE ASHEN
4. **THE ONE FOR ME** feat JAIDENE VEDA   5. **LOVE IN LUST**   6. **BLUE MOON** feat JAIDENE VEDA & KOSTNIC
7. **RÊVE** feat NAÏAD   8. **SUNRISE 2 SUNSET** feat OLU   9. **FORGIVEN** feat DEZARAY
10. **THE RIVER MIRRORS THE SKY** feat REUBEN

INNER CITY SOUND CLASH

BLUE
MOON
RÊVE

FORGIVEN

PRESS
PLAY

STILLNESS +TIME

Project
Personal

Type
Digital Illustration

In collaboration with
Tamas Arpadi

Abstract artwork can be interpreted in many different ways, leaving space for people to engage with it and find their own meanings.

For this project, I wanted to create a set of images, each using four objects to symbolise the idea of "stillness and time". I wanted the illustrations to be a snapshot of calm energy, a direct opposition to the constant barrage of images constantly presented to us online.

Basic shape sketches in Illustrator were developed in Cinema 4D. All CGI renders were created using only black and gold, and each object was made into a separate Photoshop layer with colour added using the Selective Colour adjustment layer. The key is to start in the grey channel and see how much impact you can have by tweaking individual colour channels using grey alone. Usually this helps to recolour shadows in images, and in this case, all black colour materials were able to take on bright and vibrant tones. Some people might prefer using Colour Balance instead, but I believe it doesn't provide as much accurate control over the final tonal information.

I wanted this project to be an antidote to quick test work with no extra weight behind it.

This project could have disappeared in my Instagram feed; instead, all six images were printed as giveaway postcards for design festivals, as well as a line of T-shirts.

Project
Stillness + Time

Image
Pt.2

Project
Stillness + Time

Image
Pt.3

Project
Stillness + Time

Image
Pt.5

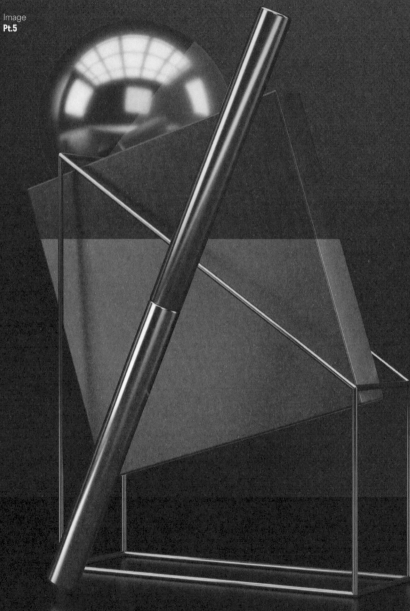

WHERE THE CITY STOPS

Client
Inhere

Type
Branding

In collaboration with
Tamas Arpadi

We never know when we'll land a dream client. When Inhere got in touch, explaining their concept of taking meditation studios to London, I took a moment to enjoy the incredible possibilities it could bring. I called them immediately, and my previous knowledge of mindfulness and meditation played a crucial part in getting the commission.

Generally, the world of wellness and meditation is filled with countless image cliches: rippling water, sunsets, horizons, impossibly toned people in yoga poses on mountaintops and the like.

After thorough conversations at the art direction strategy meetings, we decided to try to illustrate the flow of the mind. Instead of using stock imagery I reworked those cliches as icons to reflect different meanings based on the time of the day and the type of mediation. The final logo, which nods to sundials and lakes, moves with the time of the day.

The initial designs were drawn in Adobe Illustrator as multi-coloured flat illustration objects in a 16:9 ratio. We then looked into putting the "mind-flow" shapes into a spatial setting and experimented in Cinema 4D. After a few failed tests we found the right balance with a limited colour palette, which helped us focus on the shapes alone rather than needing to experiment with extra colour choices. These illustrations influenced the shape of the interior furniture and ambient lighting in the studio too, working in harmony across all touchpoints.

Given the subject of this project, I worked on every single part in self-imposed silence, allowing for total clarity and focus. Sometimes work calls for the energy loud music helps create, but this was all about balance and peace. Of course, our phones and inboxes are always clamouring for attention, but for Inhere I made every effort to enjoy the silence and keep my mind in check – adhering to what the brand stands for.

Client
Inhere

Type
**Branding
+ Design**

Client
Inhere

Image
**Branded
Flag**

inhere

smile

a ripple effect

contemplate a single
act of kindness.

———————

book online or drop in
inherestudio.com

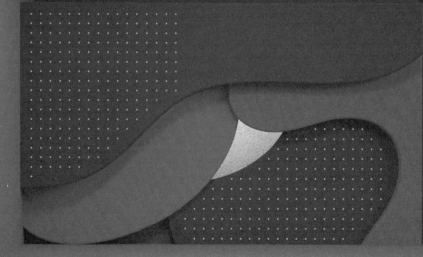

Photography
Ian Phillips-McLaren

OBJECTS IN SPACE

Client
Harnham UK

Type
**Interior design +
Graphic design**

In collaboration with
ODB Group

This project brief came in the shape of architects' drawing files. Data and analytics recruitment company Harnham's new office space wasn't much more than black architecture lines on white paper, with just seven weeks to turn that around.

Most of the heavy lifting was carried out by an established interior design company ODB Group, but it was up to me to create the environmental signage and typography for the tuck shop, set performance boards for the teams, draw abstract type-based designs for mural panels, design the entrance, create posters, assign colours for each breakout room and much more.

Making colour choices without the luxury of being able to hit Command + Z feels pretty exciting until you realise there's no easy undo. That's why you have to test ideas and think ahead around what mistakes might be made by suppliers, fitters or construction workers down the line in environmental projects like this one.

All the interior design decisions were made by putting the people who would be using the space on a daily basis first: that meant looking into possible human interactions within it, and the psychology of colours and shapes.

The goal was to bring a sense of familiarity with places we love to be in, and combine that with a place of work. Some coworking spaces mimic cafe spaces to the point of becoming a little too relaxed, and we wanted to get the balance right.

Client
Harnham UK

Photography
Jan Hlavicka

Client
Harnham UK

Photography
Jan Hlavicka

THIS IS NOT A GYM

Client
Studio 234

Type
Branding

In collaboration with
Antony Kitson
Rutger Paulusse

New gym business Studio234 wasn't more than an idea, building plan and exposed foundations when I first spoke to the founders, who were looking to create their dream studio after years of working at unhappy corporate gyms.

Since this wasn't going to be just another gym, we had to create branding that went way beyond the faceless fitness brands already out there.

The original plan was to build abstract illustrations based on celebrating the movements of the human body: twists, turns, bends and stretches were the starting point for the set of brand assets. Sadly, even after two rounds of test work, these images didn't make the right connection. It was time to change tack, so we built the brand and its assets around the 234 digits.

As the stencil shape for the logo numbers was established and signed off, we set out to fill it with meaning referencing people's movement, progress and development through training. All processing work was created with MoGraph, Soft Body Dynamics & Particles, according to the brand colour palette.

We were spoiled for choice when choosing stills from the animation – the unpredictability of the materials and interactions created some exciting, unusual results.

Stress-testing played a crucial part in visualising how the brand should come together. We created a range of trainer uniforms and exercise clothing, merchandise and accessories, all based on a brand built with 234 at the fore.

Client
S234

Type
**Bottle graphics
design**

Client
S234

Image
Animation stills

THE COLOURS OF MOODS

Project
Personal

Type
Digital Illustration

Creative Direction
Radim Malinic

Photography
Nathalie Gordon

3D
Tamas Arpadi

Stylist
Lauren Taylor

Model
Jesi Le Rae

Hair and Make Up
Bethany Garita

Colours have different associations and engender different feelings in each of us – and it can be almost impossible to describe the tone you see in your mind's eye and have someone else see it in exactly the same way.

Say "yellow" to one person and they might conjure up a lemon tone – to another, it could be anything from corn to daffodils, dandelions or butterscotch. Colours aren't just Pantone swatches – they carry unique meanings and memories for everyone.

The Colours of Moods is a conceptual collaboration with photographer Nathalie Gordon. I came up with the concept of trying to portray the nuances within colours and explore how our responses to them depend on our own emotions and environments by creating a series of colour-based images.

The aim of the project is to keep creating more of these pieces to release a project book in future.

I used a contemporary palette rather than loud, vibrant tones. The aim of the piece was to build a floor space with geometric walls either in colour harmony or contrast. Each set is based on a two-tone colour selection, expanded with other colours that can be seen as a colour thesaurus.

We exchanged ideas and mood boards for a few months before the shoot in LA. The 3D work was created in Budapest while I art directed and produced the project from London.

The whole project was produced in the space of ten days, but it took about a year to find the time to do it.

Project
The Colours of Moods

Image
PT.1

Project
The Colours of Moods

Image
PT.2

Project
The Colours of Moods

Image
PT.4

GETTING STARTED WITH ADOBE STOCK

Project
Book cover

Type
Digital illustration

In collaboration with
Adobe Stock

In commercial digital illustration, new and interesting work is always in high demand, and often in short supply. New trends quickly come and go, and often reappear cyclically as they get discarded then rediscovered by a new group of creatives. One such trend enjoying a renaissance at the moment is digital illustration in the style of oil painting. While Instagram is awash with soothing videos of paint being mixed and applied – and many artists are creating such analogue pieces to photograph and use in their work – for many of us (including myself), time, studio space and resources are too limited to experiment with oils.

This is where quick tries and fails, happy accidents and mishaps playing with stock imagery assets play a vital role in my digital illustration. The covers for both volumes of Book of Ideas were created solely from stock imagery, treating those assets so that they take on a wholly new form and meaning. To source assets, I exclusively used Adobe Stock which provides designers with access to a wonderfully diverse range of millions of curated photos, illustrations, 3D assets and loads more to give visual storytellers endless creative options. It's my go-to place thanks to many features that help to speed up my workflow.

I hadn't originally planned to release a book with abstract flower patterns on the cover, as I did with Volume I, but I followed my gut and enjoyed the unexpected results of fusing objects in contrasting colours and shapes to create something new. Stock imagery has played a crucial part in my work for more than a decade: there's something strangely satisfying when you compile a cohesive image from various pieces that sometimes don't appear to have much in common at all.

The main idea behind the cover is to continue with the abstract, vibrant theme that makes Book of Ideas the odd one out on the graphic design bookshelf. My plan is always to surprise, intrigue and slightly confuse people with what's presented to them. People judge a book by its cover more than ever now, when it's likely most people's first contact with it will be online, rather than physical. To get this book in front of people, I started with the idea of building an abstract illustration from pictures of nail varnish for the cover. I didn't stop until I had a result that ticked all the boxes.

Process
**Book cover
digital illustration**

MAKING OF
THE BOOK COVER

Project
Book cover

Type
**Digital
illustration**

In collaboration with
Adobe Stock

To get started on a project like creating the cover for this book,
you'd usually expect to spend ages on a stock website trying to find images, putting them into lightboxes and then downloading them one by one. The process used to be long, elaborate and tedious. Luckily things have moved on. Now, Adobe Stock is integrated directly within Creative Cloud apps through the Libraries menu. Uninterrupted creativity is at the heart of Adobe Stock, with a built-in search bar powered by artificial intelligence making it easier than ever to find the perfect image and keep your ideas flowing.

When I was making this cover, all my comp image searches were saved into a new Library within my Creative Cloud account. From roughly twenty images saved, I started mocking up different shapes using low-res previews. Each image was dragged directly from the Library into my Photoshop canvas, and each paint object had its white background removed to make it a transparent layer. This process provided about a dozen different shapes to play with. Once I was happy with the selection, I selected 'License Image' from the menu to download the high-res version for each stock image. It's a great feature that replaces your watermarked low-res images with high-resolution files that are ready to use the moment you license them. I didn't have to leave Photoshop for a second – the process was completed entirely through Adobe Stock integration.

Each paint stock layer was then recoloured using Hue and Saturation to give it the most vibrant and rich look within a colour palette of tones that compliment each other. The detailed texture in the varnish paint gives extra detail to work with, so when I settled on the final layout, I exported the image as a flat JPEG to apply the Oil Brush filter across all elements. To achieve the desired painterly aesthetic, I hit the filter three times until I got the look right. This technique gives all the original stock images more of an ownable look and feel by blending elements together.
-
Adobe Stock has curated the images used here to give you the opportunity to follow along and make your own abstract illustration to suit the covers in the Book of Ideas series. Download the original assets to get started.
adobe.com/go/bookofideas

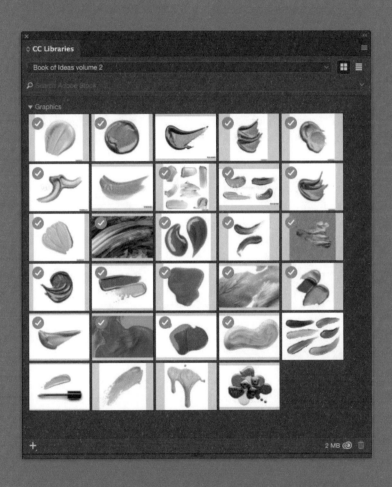

Process
**Adobe Stock image
selection**

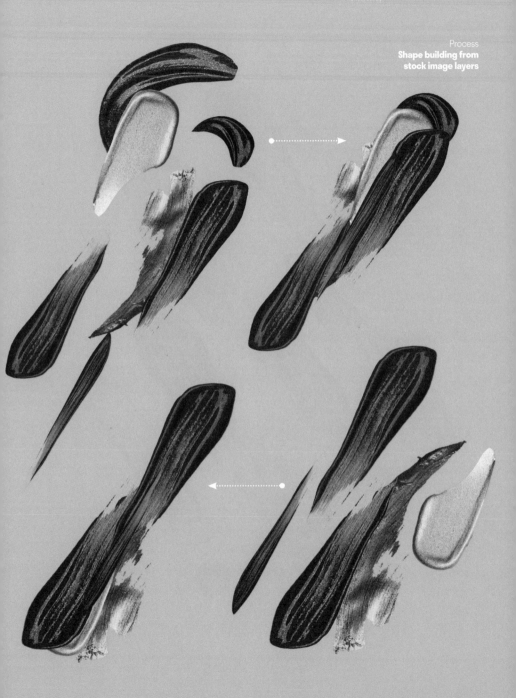

Process
**Shape building from
stock image layers**

Process
Basic layer version

Process
Oil paint filter applied

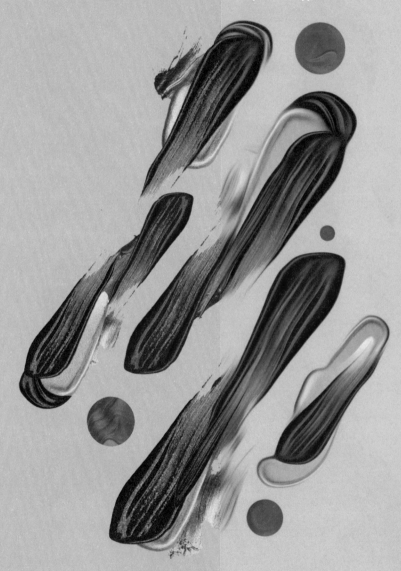

book
of ideas

A journal of creative direction
and graphic design

Radim Malinic

Volume 2

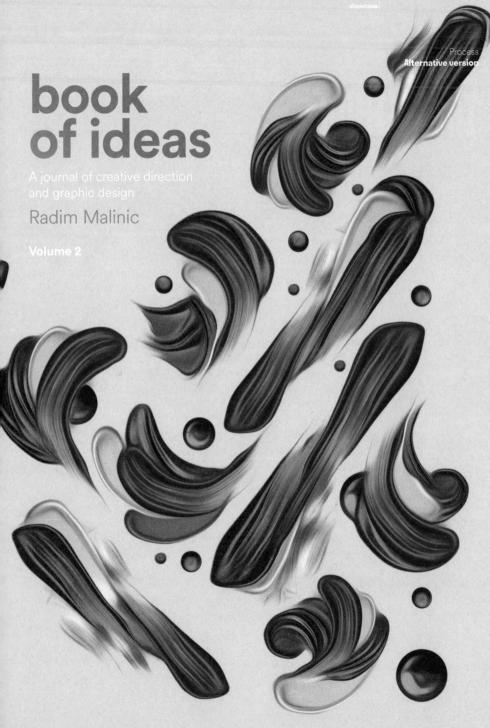

ABOUT THE AUTHOR

Radim Malinic is a creative director and designer living and working in South West London. He runs Brand Nu® an award winning studio. Taking a multidisciplinary approach, he works across creative direction, design, illustration, typography, product design and music video direction to form a practice based around positivity, message and meaning.

Before finding his calling in the creative industry, Czech born Malinic was an ice hockey player, a bassist in death metal bands, an indie DJ, music journalist and student of Economics and Business management.

At the break of the new millennium, Malinic moved to the United Kingdom to explore the expansive music scene, only to find even an greater interest in art and graphic design. Since then his eclectic interests have seen him working with some of the biggest brands, companies and bands in the world. Clients include Harry Potter Platform 9 3/4, 007 Store, Coca Cola, Google, Adobe Systems, WWF and USAID amongst many others. Whatever the project, Radim's central belief is to help his clients achieve their objective by delivering the best work possible.

Aside from his studio work, Radim designs products for his brand 'November Universe', releases music and tours design events and universities globally with his talks and lectures designed to inspire and support self-development in the creative industry.

In March 2016, Malinic released his publication, Book of Ideas. The Amazon #1 Graphic Arts bestseller has helped novices and professionals across the world to find a new way of approaching their creative work.

Radim was born in 1978 in Frydek-Mistek in the Czech Republic, and has been based in the United Kingdom since 2000.

Photography
Jan Hlavicka

THANKS AND ACKNOWLEDGEMENTS

I am thankful that I can keep meeting new people, friends, collaborators and inspiring souls ...

Aaron Draplin, Aaron Martin, Aaron Phipps, Ade Mills, Adhemas Batista, Adiba Osmani, Adolfo Ferreira, Adrian Mills, Adrien Gervaix, Alan Wardle, Alberto Garcia Corroto, Alessandro Scotto, Alex Donne-Johnsson, Alex Hewitt, Alex Kerman, Alex Mathers, Alex Suchet, Alfred Park, Alvaro Salas Herrera, Alyce Calkins, Amit Soni, Andreas Bierwirth, Andrew Logo Creative, Andy Potts, Anna Mullin, Anne Wollenberg, Anthea Mccourtie, Antony Kitson, Arthur Lewin, Ash Thorpe, Ava Mahdavi, Bea Mk, Ben Edwards, Bikie Isharaza And Debs Isharaza, Billy Bogiatzoglou, Blue Deer Design - Mark Hirons, Bram Timmer, Brandin' You, Cameron Duthie, Caroline Brealey, Cedric Schoenecker, Chanelle Studwick, Charlie Sells, Che Mcpherson, Chelsie Sixsmith, Chris Alexander, Chris Anderson, Chris Arran, Chris Olimpo, Chris Page, Chris Venables, Chuck Anderson, Claudia Beatrice Vergine, Craig Minchington, Daniel Clark, Daniel Maw, Daniel Nelson, David Carson, David Delahay, David Delin, David Farmer, David Nuff, David Sheldon Hicks, David Stephen, David Stypka, Design In Delft - Hello Frank! Dines & Blup Fam, Dominic Wilcox, Ed Baigrie, Ed Baptist, Edoardo Rainoldi, Ella Tomlin Kedge, Ellen Hancock, Emily Gosling, Emma Axling, Emma Foster, Fabien Barral, Fabio Sasso, Francois Hoang, Franz Jeitz, Gareth Martindale, Garry Kincaid, Gavin Strange, George Smerin, Georgia Archer, Glen John Jones, Gmunk, Gordon Reid, Green Tea Visions, Greg Browne, Hanna Nilsson, Harry Roberts, Hector Ayuso, Isaiah Haakmat, Jac Poole, Jack Harries, Jacob Anderson, James Collingwood, James White, Jennifer Proudler, Johan Lindh, Johann Chan, John Deane, Jonathan Ball, Jonathan Sands, Jonnathan Olmos Wilches, Jonny Greene, Julien Vallée, Juliette Hettema, Jürgen Rosenauer, Justina Bogdaite, Karoly Kiralyfalvi, Kate Dawkins, Katerina Lyadova, Katie Knecht, Katie Lang, Kelvin Yap, Kerry Roper, Kevin Bishop, Krysta Youngs, Kyle So, Kyle Wilkinson, Laura Jane Boast, Lauren Hom, Leo Marti, Leslie Hardcastle, Liam Miller, Linda Ayton, Lindsay Dixon,

Lizzy Mary Cullen, Lloyd Evans, Loic Sattler, Lubomir Abrinko, Lucy Kitchen, Luke Freeman, Luke Whitaker, Maciej Hajnrich, Marcel Mölter, Marcin Molski, Marcus Headicar, Mariah Anden, Marija Zlotnikova, Mark Best, Mark Cooper, Mark Ford, Mark Thiele, Marta Jackwiewicz, Mat Macquarrie, Matt Mccue, Matthew Potter, Melanie Khan, Michael Cina, Michale Chaize, Mike Harrison, Mike Winkleman Aka Beeple, Minimal S.r.l.s., Morten Ols, Mr Bingo, Naomi Atkinson, Natalia Bertok, Natalie Koutia, Nathalie Gordon, Nathan Kemp, Nawfal Rihani, Nayade Bermudez Brito, Neil Bennett, Nic Yeeles, Nicole Feeney, Nina Sans & Rafa Goicoechea, Omar Vega, P.l Vonk, Parker Gibson, Patrick Broekhuizen, Paul Berthelon Bravo, Paul Ridney, Paul Seager, Paul Skeffington, Pete Harrison, Peter Appleton, Peter Jaworowski, Philip Goodeve-Docker, Philip Meagher, Rachel Lamb, Radim Houfek, Rahul Bhatt, Rahul Bhatt, Rik Oostenbroek, Rizon Parein, Rob Braithwaite, Rob Clark, Rob Jelinski Studios, Rob Quirk, Robert Bakker, Rodrigo Machado, Roger Daoud, Rufus Deuchler, Rutger Pauluse, Ryan Cook, Saad Moosajee, Sam Gilbey, Sarah Ellen Masters, Seb Lester, Sebastian Spasic, Shawn Pucknell, Shiyam Sritharan, Sian Horn, Simon Clarke, Simon Edwards, Šimon Halaj, Simon Kenyon, Soy Mustafa, Stefan Sagmeister, Stephen Mccleery, Steven Bonner, Tamas Arpadi, Tammi Heals, Tash Wilcocks, Thain Lurk, Thi Hoang, Thorsten Klein, Tiago Ribeiro, Tim Dye, Tim Harper, Toby Vane, Tom Muller, Tom Shoene, Tomas Trcka, Tony Harmer, Tony Wiley Deesign, Victor Bergnale, Wakar Khan, Wayne Johns and Yael Levey.

Made in partnership with **Adobe Stock** and **Adobe Creative Cloud**

Thanks to my family Eva, Sandra, Laura and Ellie.

Eternal love and gratitude go to my wife **Rachel** for putting up with my crazy ideas, keeping me sane in moments of panic, not even trying to laugh at my bad jokes. I let her steal my socks so I guess we are even?! Thank you for being incredible.

This book is dedicated to my daughter **Harper Lux Freda** - she's a daily ray of sunshine in our family life. I feel blessed to share my life moments with such a beautiful and gentle soul. Love you!